GETTING THE RIGHT THINGS DONE

The Habit of Putting First Things First

ROMUALD ANDRADE

GETTING THE **RIGHT** THINGS **DONE**
© Romuald Andrade 2016

First Edition 2016

Published in India by:
Embassy Book Distributors
120, Great Western Building,
Maharashtra Chamber of Commerce Lane,
Fort, Mumbai 400 023, India
Tel: (+9122) -30967415, 22819546
Email: info@embassybooks.in
www.embassybooks.in

ISBN: 978-93-85492-93-8

*All rights reserved. No part of this publication may
be reproduced, distributed, or transmitted in any
form or by any means, including photocopying,
recording, or other electronic or mechanical methods,
without the prior written permission of the publisher.
The use of brief quotations embodied in reviews is
permitted.*

Layout and typesetting by PSV Kumarasamy

Printed : SAP Print Solutions Pvt. Ltd., Mumbai

Contents

SECTION I

Chapter 1	7
Chapter 2	13
Chapter 3	23
Chapter 4	33
Chapter 5	45
Chapter 6	51
Chapter 7	59
Chapter 8	67
Chapter 9	73
Chapter 10	77
Chapter 11	81
Chapter 12	89
Chapter 13	91
Chapter 14	95
Chapter 15	101
Chapter 16	109
Chapter 17	117
Chapter 18	121
Chapter 19	125
Chapter 20	129

SECTION II

Getting the RIGHT things done	137
Vision	147
The Weekly Review	153
The Daily Plan	157
Key Concepts	161
Getting Ready	167
Conclusion	173
Your Free Gift	175

Section 1

Chapter 1

Steve wheeled his car out of his parking spot at MobileTech. He anxiously glanced at the clock on the dashboard. "Damn," he chastised himself. It was already 3:50. The funeral service was supposed to start at 4:00, and he was surely going to be late.

He decided to quickly pull over before he left to send his girlfriend a text message saying he was on his way. He told himself he didn't want to interrupt her time with family with a phone call, but he had to admit it was also an excuse to avoid having to tell her he hadn't even gotten on the road yet.

There was only one good thing that had ever happened to him in his life, and her name was Sue Amadori. His one true love, really. Sure, he had a girlfriend back in college, but it was different with Sue.

She was five feet two inches of pure mischief. She had tan skin and eyes that could hypnotize you. He loved that girl.

But just like every other aspect of his life, the course of their love had not run smoothly.

He knew he should have left earlier. Actually, Sue had asked him not to go in at all. She knew his work habits, and she had worried he would be late to the funeral. He had reassured her that all would be fine, and now look at him.

He felt just awful. But as he had explained to Sue, today was the big meeting. Steve, his boss Jeff, and even Jeff's boss Al, the CTO, had been expected in the boardroom at 9 a.m. sharp.

The meeting had gone well, but had also gone well over the expected time frame, as they usually did. When Steve tried to excuse himself at 3:00 to make it to the service, Jeff and Al were still deep in conversation, brainstorming and reviewing their options.

They kept asking him questions and obviously it was not possible for him to leave just then. It seemed those two were never done with work, and Steve couldn't help but wonder what their home lives were like.

As he started the car again, his phone started ringing. He picked it up as he started to drive.

"You had to text me!" Sue said. "Why didn't you call? Where are you?"

"On my way, sweetheart, I'm in the car."

"You're on the freeway?"

Steve tried to navigate the parking lot with one hand. "Almost. I'll be there in half an hour."

"The service starts in ten minutes, Steve," she whispered angrily, obviously trying to keep her voice low and her temper in check because of her surroundings.

"I cannot believe you are doing this. Not now. Not today."

"I know, I know..."

"No! You don't know! It's bad enough Joey had to bring me and Vito to the funeral when it should have been you here to support us. But I agreed to that because I knew today was an important day for you. But what about me? This is one of the saddest days of my life, and you aren't even here with me..."

Sue's voice trailed off and Steve could hear her beginning to quietly cry. "Sue, I'm so sorry," Steve swallowed the lump growing in his throat.

"I'll be there as quickly as I can be," he said, bracing himself as he said so.

"Ok." Sue's voice was barely audible as she hung up. She wiped her tears away and tried to stay strong for her grandfather, Vito Vitale. He and her grandmother had taken her in after her parents had been killed in a car accident.

She had been young and alone, and they were all she had. They were her world then and they still were now. She had even insisted that Steve buy a home close to them so she would never have to be without them. They had raised her, loved her, and taken care of her when there was no one else.

Sue had vowed she would never leave them alone, and felt that now it was her turn to take care of them whenever they needed her. She had seen them every day without fail, either by visiting them at their home or by going out for lunch.

But today... today was one of the worst days Sue could remember in a long time. Her grandmother Sarah lay silent in the coffin as her grandfather tried to stay strong. Her grandparents had been together for more years than she could count. They had emigrated from Italy together to make a better life for themselves and their children in America.

They had provided for her in so many ways, and to think her grandmother was gone now... it was too much. The least she could have hoped was that Steve would be here for both her and Vito.

Sue shook her head, gave a final dab at her eyes, and straightened up. No, she wasn't going to let her grandfather see her this way. If Steve

GETTING THE **RIGHT** THINGS DONE 11

wasn't going to be here for support, then she had to be strong for both of them.

She looked at her watch. It was 4:00, and the service was starting. Time to be strong.

As he drove, Steve kept thinking about what a disappointment he was to Sue. Sue, with her huge brown eyes and long dark hair. The last thing Steve wanted to do was let her down at a time like this.

And of course that's exactly what he had done. All he wanted to do was provide for her and take care of her, but he seemed to disappoint her more and more lately. After what seemed like an eternity of fighting traffic and hitting every red light on the streets, Steve pulled into the cemetery.

Steve was out of breath as he sprinted through the cemetery lawns. He spotted Sue and Vito and pushed through the small group to make his way to her side.

Steve took Sue's small hand in his and gently kissed her cheek. She turned to look at him, and Steve immediately knew he had messed up badly.

They listened to the priest's eulogy while the casket slowly dropped into the ground. The priest gave his final blessing, and the mourners tossed dirt onto the grave one by one and slowly filed off the cemetery premises.

After the funeral, Sue's cousin Joey took Vito home.

Steve and Sue left the cemetery together, and drove home in silence.

"I'm so sorry," Steve murmured, hoping to get Sue to speak to him. "Not just about today. About everything. I'm so sorry for you and your grandfather. I wish I had been there for you." Sue didn't respond, but wiped away a tear as it rolled down her cheek. Steve wondered if it was possible to actually, physically feel your heart break.

After a silent and mostly sleepless night, Steve's alarm went off at 5:30 a.m. as usual. He quietly got out of bed, leaving Sue sleeping quietly. He knew it would be another long day at the office, but wondered how much he would really be able to focus on work.

Chapter 2

MobileTech was located in Santa Clara County, California.

It used to have all the trappings of a Silicon Valley company, the Detroit of the 21st century. It had the most experienced engineers in the mobile applications space, an expensive executive team with venture capital firms lining up to invest, and talented engineers straight out of college vying to get in.

But that was a very long time ago. Good engineers were now in short supply and tended to regard themselves as elite, with the best being paid six-figure bonuses just to stay on at companies such as Google and Facebook. No experienced engineer would be willing to consider MobileTech now!

MobileTech started out by providing development services in the mobility space on Android, iOS, and mobile web-based solutions.

Their healthcare and travel apps were in huge demand until copycat apps began to appear in the marketplace.

The company had been experiencing many setbacks ever since one of the technical co-founders moved out to start another venture. Critical deadlines started to slip. A few key engineers unexpectedly left the company. Morale deteriorated gradually.

The end result of these setbacks was that the company was acquired by FireStorm, Inc. in a stock and cash deal in excess of $1 billion.

FireStorm, Inc. was a publicly listed cyber security company which was into development of web application firewall products.

The company did not seem to be any better under the new management. Steve had the responsible position of a Project Manager but he was not sure if he was on the right track with his career due to current developments. He was not the best among the engineers but he made up for his shortcomings by being extremely hard-working and putting in extra hours at work. He got promoted a year ago, when he turned 26. His team had a mix of senior and junior engineers.

Steve's team was always on tight deadlines, and Steve was finding it difficult not to pass on the stress from the boardroom to his subordinates while getting the job done. In the process, he

GETTING THE **RIGHT** THINGS **DONE**   15

found himself increasingly stuck in the middle and stressed out!

Just a week earlier, a top-level team from FireStorm, Inc. had come in to discuss the problems with the current merger. Rumor had it that they had proposed a 'flat-management structure,' which meant that Steve's job could become redundant.

Steve, looking for a solution to this problem, assumed that if he improved his own productivity, then the company would recognize his contributions. Perhaps he could even move up higher on the food chain.

This morning promised to be different. Steve and his team were ready to show a demo of their proposed app to the management team.

Perhaps this was the day that Steve would finally be able to make a good impression with the management team. As soon as Steve entered the office, he dropped off his bag and headed straight for Bob's cubicle first. Bob Burton was a senior engineer in Steve's team. Bob spoke very little, but whenever he did, he had something important and constructive to say. He listened intently during meetings, worked long hours with no complaint, and helped the junior engineers with debugging their applications.

Bob had already kept 6 mobile phones ready for the demo with the app installed on all of them. Steve was pleased to see that everything was ready and he grabbed 3 of the phones in one hand and asked Bob to carry the rest of them. His next destination was his boss's office.

As he approached, Steve could see that the cabin door was open. His boss, Jeff Gilmore, was sitting behind his desk, working on his computer.

Steve knocked and came in without waiting for a response. Bob followed closely behind him.

"Excuse me."

Jeff looked up. "Steve Payton," he exclaimed. "You'd better have some good news for me!"

"All good, Jeff," Steve said with a grin.

"Is that the app?" asked Jeff, pointing to the phones that Steve was carrying.

"Yes, Bob has loaded them on all the phones for the demo."

"Okay then." Jeff grabbed his notebook. "Let's go."

Steve was accustomed to Jeff's get-to-the-point approach. Jeff was from an application development background and did not have expertise in mobile development prior to joining MobileTech. In the last 3 years, Jeff had been responsible for standardizing the processes in order to help each of the seven teams under him meet their deadlines.

GETTING THE **RIGHT** THINGS DONE   17

While the process alignment worked, the high staff turnover and the lack of a winning product made Jeff nervous. Steve's new idea for a product seemed to be exactly what he needed to turn the company around.

Steve and Bob followed Jeff to the conference room where they found the four executives were already seated.

Jeff took the seat at the end of the conference table opposite Martin Perlow, the CEO. Martin was from a finance background and he had started MobileTech in association with Nick Campbell, the former CTO. Nick and Martin had a falling out, which led to Martin buying out Nick's shares in the company two years ago and Nick moving out to start another venture.

To his right was the CFO, Amanda Goldberg, and to his left was the VP of Sales and Marketing, Ross Turner. Sitting next to Amanda was the CTO, Al Rawlins who seemed to be very busy typing out something on his laptop.

Bob went around the room distributing the phones to everyone. The meeting started off with Steve simulating a phone call with one of the demo phones to the phone which was with Ross Turner. Immediately the name 'Steve Payton' flashed on the screen.

"So what is this app?" asked Ross. "Is it a caller ID app?"

"Well, yes... but it does much more than just that," replied Steve. "Do any of you get unsolicited phone calls in-spite of being on the DND (Do not Disturb) Registry?"

There was a chorus of murmured yeses in the room.

"Well, this app is a solution for that," said Steve. "You see, when someone gets a call from an unknown number, he usually picks it up just to see who it is because the number is not stored in his contact list. This app eliminates the need to pick up each and every phone call by informing you who is calling."

"I get a lot of calls like that, but I simply don't pick them up," said Amanda. "Why do you need an app for that?"

"Most users are curious and therefore feel they have to pick up calls from unknown numbers," said Steve. "Our solution basically creates a phone-book in the cloud by crowdsourcing information from other users of the app, who have previously saved the phone number as a telemarketing number or as spam."

"But doesn't that mean that you need a certain number of initial users in order to make this viable?" The question was from Al Rawlins, who did not seem interested in his laptop anymore.

Before Steve could reply, Amanda chimed in. "And what are you planning to charge for this app?"

GETTING THE **RIGHT** THINGS DONE   19

Steve decided to address both questions. "We were thinking of offering the app for free until we got a certain number of users, after which it would go viral--"

"Seriously! Go viral - that's your strategy?" - The comment was from Ross Turner, who did not look pleased. "Can you name any one app that your team has built that has gone viral, Steve?"

Steve was silent for a few seconds while he collected his thoughts, but Ross was not done. "So what is the market size for this app?" he asked.

Steve fumbled while he answered Ross's question.

"I don't know Ross .... this is just a demo app ..."

"Are you targeting any particular geography?"

"Apart from the number of users, how will you measure your success?"

"Have you created any personas of your target audience?"

Ross peppered Steve with questions until Martin spoke.

"Whoa, hold on Ross!" said Martin. "I think everyone should just take a fifteen minute break while Steve figures this one out." He nodded at Jeff. "Jeff, I think you should help Steve out on this one - we will convene in another fifteen minutes."

The management team shuffled out of the room with Martin being the last to leave. Hearing the door creak shut behind Martin, Jeff spoke to Bob. "Bob, I think we would not require your help beyond this point. I would suggest that you should continue working on the Blackberry project you were working on earlier."

When Bob left, Jeff turned his full attention to Steve. "What do you think went wrong?" He asked Steve.

Steve looked down at his feet. "I just don't know Jeff" He finally replied, "I thought it was a good idea!"

"It is a great idea, and it was YOUR idea - but you did not present it well!" said Jeff.

Steve nodded as Jeff continued, "If you can buy some more time from them, what will you do differently this time?"

"I would probably hire a market research agency to do a study on the viability of this project." said Steve

"That may be a solution but we will have to figure out how we are going to convince them today!" said Jeff. "Let's grab a cup of coffee while we figure this one out!"

Jeff and Steve headed over to the coffee machine and discussed several aspects of the project on their way back. When everyone

GETTING THE **RIGHT** THINGS DONE   21

eventually trickled back into the room almost fifteen minutes later, Martin asked Steve to present again.

This time Steve stepped over to the whiteboard and using a marker wrote out:

'Development Plan | Marketing Plan | Monetization Plan'

He then proceeded to explain that while he did not have a marketing plan and monetization plan ready, he was very confident that his team could develop a beta version of the app in 3 months given their current commitments.

Everyone had questions about the features of the app and opinions about how it would be received in the market.

"Is anyone really going to buy this?" asked Amanda.

"What are the current alternatives to this app?" asked Ross.

"None that we know of" said Jeff

"Okay, but will people buy it?" asked Amanda again

Conscious of the time, Martin interrupted. "We can have this conversation another time. Don't forget that Steve and Jeff are engineers not marketers. Let's move on to the timeline."

Steve remained standing and quickly drew out the development timeline, breaking it down by week and month.

Martin cautioned Steve, "I like the fact that you know your development stuff, Steve, but you need to realize that as a project manager, you also have to consider things like the budget of the app. It also would not hurt you to learn a bit more from Ross and Amanda about how this app could be marketed and monetized."

Martin went on to talk about how an app should be disruptive and should "change the world." Steve thought Martin considered himself the next Steve Jobs. Martin ended the meeting by asking Steve to present his project plan on Monday morning.

Chapter 3

Steve needed another cup of coffee after that meeting! He knew he had been prepared; he had read his notes over and over again, and knew exactly what he wanted to say. "Then why did you freeze like that?" he asked himself as he walked out of the conference room, using a tissue to wipe the sweat from his forehead.

He headed over to his desk and realized he had forgotten to grab a cup of coffee from the vending machine. Shaking his head, he turned around and walked back to the vending machine to get his coffee.

This was not the first time that something like this had happened to him. He was forgetting appointments, losing important papers, freezing up in meetings, and worst of all, he had shown up late for Sue's grandmother's funeral.

That had been the worst thing yet. He shuddered, remembering the disappointment in

Sue's eyes and the way she had tried to remain strong for herself and her grandfather, but had really needed him there.

Steve tried to distract himself from these thoughts by taking a sip of the hot, bitter coffee. Before long, Steve arrived at his desk. Well, he was pretty sure there was a desk there, but he hadn't seen it in a long time. Someone could have replaced it with a cardboard box and he would never know the difference. The desk was littered with papers, clips, and other office supplies. The walls of his cubicle were a mess in their own right. Outdated memos and other trash remained pinned to the soft walls of the nook, and the result was a feeling that the walls were closing in on him.

Steve was still considering what he should have said in the meeting he just came from and wasn't paying attention to where he was going.

It was at that point that Steve tripped on his chair and spilled his coffee all over the papers strewn about his desk. In a panic, Steve did everything he could to wipe up the mess and salvage the important papers. Of course, in that stack of paperwork, it was impossible to tell which items were a priority. Soaking wet with coffee stains, there was no way to sort through anything.

Cursing under his breath, he grabbed a paper towel and started mopping up the spill, knocking

GETTING THE **RIGHT** THINGS DONE   25

off some of the important post-it notes that were stuck to his computer monitor.

As he stepped back to examine his handiwork, it hit him. His desk was as messy as his life. The haphazard pile of books, the three half-filled coffee mugs, the monitor full of post-it notes, the stockpile of folders with papers jutting out screaming for his attention, and what he could only assume was old sandwich wrappers.

"Damn," he whispered, and sat down heavily in his chair. Exasperated, he ran a hand through his hair, and wondered if this was what Sue saw when she looked at him. Good intentions with no direction.

After a while, even good intentions can become lost in the mess. Steve began thinking about Martin and His Steve Jobs quotes - how could he change the world when he could not even change his own desk!

In the chaos, Steve again considered how his desk was a metaphor for everything else in his life in the recent past. Like the soggy papers in his hands, it seemed like his life was falling apart right in front of him.

He sank down into his chair wishing that he could just get up, leave the office, and head home. But what good would that do? Sue was as annoyed with him as he was with himself. He needed to make some changes, but he was too overwhelmed to figure out where to begin.

As he sat staring at the blank screen in defeat, he heard a voice behind him. "Whoa! What happened here?" It was Sean "Superman" Watkins, who was also a project manager and a good friend. In fact, it was Sean who had referred Steve to MobileTech.

When he realized Sean was standing behind him, he stammered, "I just spilled my coffee, and I... I... I don't know what to do, man, my life is a mess, and my desk is worse." Hearing himself confess, he turned a bright shade of red, and beads of sweat began to appear on his face.

He looked down at his hands, shocked that he had blurted out so much even though Sean was a good friend. Maybe he should not have said that. "Gimme a minute," said Sean, walking away. Sean returned a few minutes later with a book titled 'Zap Your Procrastination.'

Sean spoke up and said, "I get it man, all of this can get overwhelming, but this book helped me a lot, and maybe it can do the same for you."

Steve was unsure how to respond. He didn't think that a book was what he needed but he knew that Sean was just trying to help.

"Thanks, Sean."

Steve paged through the book, hoping it contained at least a few good tips he might put to use. He wanted to be optimistic, but was fairly convinced a book couldn't get the disaster he called his life back on track.

"I'll give it a read," he said, giving Sean a half-smile.

Just then, Steve's phone rang. Jeff was calling requesting an update on the progress of another project. Seeing the immediate tension in Steve's face, Sean placed a kind hand on his shoulder and excused himself. "Thanks again," Steve whispered to Sean, covering the receiver with his hand as he struggled to focus on the questions Jeff was throwing at him all at once.

Once Steve had promised Jeff that he would get back to him with the most recent statistics and other information he had requested, he hung up the phone and glanced at the book Sean gave him. Dubious, but willing to try anything at this point, he decided to take a few minutes to read at least the first chapter.

But before he could reach for the book, he heard someone calling out to him.

"Steve."

He looked up to see Janice, one of his engineers approaching his desk

"Jeff is asking for the document you were working on last week for the Blackberry Project. Did you finish it?"

Steve's mind began racing. He had completed the project during one of his late-night sessions last week; hadn't he given it to Jeff already? No, evidently it was one more thing he had forgotten to do. "It's finished," Steve replied, nervously beginning to dig through the pile of papers on his desk. "It's here somewhere.."

"It's ok, Steve," Janice said, giving him an empathetic smile. "I'll tell Jeff you're putting the finishing touches on it. Just give me a call when you find it and I'll hand it over to him."

"Ok," Steve nodded, rummaging through the seemingly never-ending pile of paperwork. As Janice returned to her work station, Steve felt himself flushing with both embarrassment and frustration. He knew his co-workers viewed him as a disorganized klutz; they had to, since that was how he viewed himself.

After another 20 minutes of searching his desk and encountering documents dated over six months ago, Steve finally realized that he might have misplaced the document. "Damn it," he muttered to himself. Leaning back in his chair and running a hand through his hair, Steve knew it was going to be another late night. Make that a number of late nights. Many of the graphs wouldn't have been saved in the right folders on his computer, so he was going to have to redo most of them, which was the most time-consuming part of the project. Furious with himself, he closed his eyes and tried to remain calm. "Man," he muttered to himself. "You better get it together..."

After another two weeks of late nights, playing catch-up, and trying to stay on track, Steve decided one morning that he needed to make the time to clean up his desk. He didn't have time, but after that last stunt he had pulled with the Blackberry Project, he knew he'd better make it a priority.

After an hour or so of filing what he needed and shredding what he didn't, Steve's desk was starting to look a bit more manageable. As he dug into yet another pile of paper, his fingers hit something solid. Pushing aside the top of the pile, he found himself staring at the book Sean had given him. "I forgot all about this," he whispered to himself, tracing the title with his fingers.

Over the next few days, Steve couldn't put the book down. In fact, he found himself carrying the book with him everywhere. He was pulling it out during his lunch hour and even reading a chapter or two each night before going to sleep.

He felt his mood beginning to brighten with each turn of the page. When he finally finished the book, he decided to put it into action right away. He grabbed a few boxes from the office storage area and the recycling box and got started.

He started out by labeling the boxes using a thick marker. He removed all the items on his desk except for the computer and the telephone and moved them onto the floor of his cubicle next to the boxes.

He moved the stapler, pens, pencils, etc. into the 'stationary box.' He found a lot of items that were no longer needed and promptly pitched them into the recycling bin.

While sifting through the papers he also found a lot of papers that were related to other members of his team. So he quickly grabbed a marker, labeled an empty box with "Other people" and started moving things to this box.

He had now managed to clear off both the top area of his desk as well as the piles on the floor, so he decided to keep up the momentum and cleared out the desk drawers and cabinets and moved the items into new piles on the floor. He was soon able to find a place for everything and was pleased to see that everything was in its place.

The feeling he got when he was finally able to see his desk was greater than anything he felt in a long time.

For the first time in a month, Steve felt like he had things under control and was finally able to get his thoughts as organized as his desk. Over the next few days, he received praise from co-workers regarding his work, and Jeff also commented on the great ideas he presented at the next meeting.

He no longer felt claustrophobic sitting in his cube.

It was truly a mystery. How on earth had organizing his desk led to organizing his thoughts?

Steve couldn't believe the effect his organized desk had on his productivity...

Chapter 4

A few days later, as Steve sat at his somewhat cleared desk, he gazed at the newly placed picture of him and Sue standing in front of a waterfall at Yosemite. Amazed at the calming effect of the photo, he marvelled at the difference in his mood this past week. Since implementing the tips in the book, he had noticed several changes. Not only had his spirit improved considerably, but he believed his level of productivity has also increased significantly.

Of course, Steve was not so arrogant as to think his issues were completely solved. He was still working longer hours than most people; his desk, while much neater than before, could still be better organized, and his home life... well, he was working on it.

"Good morning, Steve," Sean gave a quick nod as he walked by, one hand filled with paperwork, and a cup of coffee in the other.

"Hey Sean," Steve responded. As always, Steve was impressed with the ease with which Sean seemed to breeze through life. Approximately the same age as Steve, and in the same position of project manager, Sean seemed to be the poster child of happiness and success.

Steve knew Sean's team respected him tremendously, and their level of output was phenomenal. In fact, Sean had won the best project manager award multiple times. Sean's engineers were not better trained than his own, nor were they any different in terms of work ethic. Both teams had good workers, yet Sean's team seemed to always do better than all the other teams in the company.

And perhaps most notably, they did this without working an excessive number of late nights. Actually, Steve didn't remember Sean's team ever working past 6:00 p.m. It was at that moment Steve realized Sean might be a good mentor after whom he could model himself.

In the past, Steve would have been embarrassed to consider such a thing. After all, Sean and Steve had the same background, experience, and education. No, it wasn't that Steve needed Sean to teach him the job; nothing as simple as that. He needed Sean to teach him life skills. Ok, that was a weird thought. Why would a grown man need a peer to teach him about life? Steve reddened a bit at the thought of asking Sean for help, and shook his head. But really, what was the harm?

GETTING THE **RIGHT** THINGS DONE   35

Steve rubbed his chin with his hand, his mind and heart racing at the thought of asking for help. "Oh, just do it," he murmured to himself. As Steve approached Sean's cubicle, he instantly noticed the tidiness and organization in Sean's work area, and made a mental note that he would continue to work on his own space. Baby steps, he reminded himself.

"Hey Steve," Sean smiled. "How's life in the world of mobile apps?"

"Well," Steve shook his head, "It's been challenging, to say the least." Sean nodded his head in understanding, and having been there himself, he truly did understand.

Sean had been in a similar position several months ago, with short deadlines and high expectations to deliver a complex product. Again, Steve realized the big difference was the ease with which Sean had handled the situation.

With a quick sweep of the office, Steve noted that nobody was close enough to be within earshot, so he took a deep breath and summoned up his courage.

"Sean, I have a big, and... well... kind of an odd favor to ask of you." Intrigued, Sean put down the document he had been holding, swivelled his chair in Steve's direction, and tilted his head in anticipation.

Steve again touched his chin, one of the signs that he was nervous or uncomfortable. "See, being in the same position, I know you understand exactly what I go through here... the pressure, the heavy workload... managing a team…" he trailed off, carefully considering his next words.

As Sean nodded in empathy, Steve was encouraged to continue. "I appreciate and admire the way you work. You are able to handle a lot of work. You never seem to be flustered, no matter what's going on around here. And man, you never work a late night!"

Sean chuckled at the last statement. "Oh, I do. Sometimes I even take work home with me."

"Ok, I know sometimes it's inevitable," Steve went on, "but seriously, you seem to have it all sorted out. I know this sounds strange, but I was wondering if you could help me, you know, kind of like a mentor..." again, trailing off, as he shifted from one foot to another.

"Steve, it would be my pleasure to work with you," Sean interrupted in an attempt to put Steve at ease. "I'm flattered you think so highly of me. We all question ourselves, and when you hear someone else thinks you're doing it right, well... that's something." Sean smiled.

Steve breathed a sigh of relief, "Thanks man, I would really appreciate any advice you have."

Sean smiled again, "The first thing we're going to work on are your organizational habits. Tell you what: grab a chair and let's talk now. I want

GETTING THE **RIGHT** THINGS DONE 37

you to spend some time shadowing me every day, watching how I structure my workday... you know, some of the basic stuff."

As Steve looked around for an extra chair, he thanked Sean, "That would be great, thank you so much."

Sean winked. "Don't thank me yet. I'm a tough evaluator."

Steve chuckled, knowing Sean was probably serious. "Sounds good to me," he said, as he grabbed a chair and made his way back to Sean's cubicle. "I look forward to the evaluations."

Sean asked what he was currently doing with the team, to which Steve replied that he simply gave them the work plan and the timeline as to when the mobile app should be ready for presentation to the senior management. He also checked in with them frequently to see how they were doing.

Sean smiled. "Those are definitely the most important things, but let's take it a step further. For starters, ask the team how they would like to be managed. Obviously, they're all professionals. They know their jobs and what they're setting out to accomplish. Your main focus should be their management needs. Your team is already aware of your strengths and weaknesses, so they're in the best position to give you feedback."

Steve knit his brow in thought. "That's true," he nodded. "I hadn't really thought of it that way."

Sean nodded and continued, "Treat engineers as partners and listen to their thoughts on the project plans. Obviously you'll want to keep track of their progress, but remember, they are professionals, so give them their space. I mean, let's face it," he smiled, "Anyone with the tenacity to earn a degree in Engineering doesn't typically require micro-management."

Chuckling, Steve agreed. "Alright," he nodded. "Thanks for taking some time with me. I'm getting a clearer picture of what I need to do in regards to my team."

Sean extended his hand. As Steve took it, he suggested, "Let's meet back here tomorrow for a follow-up."

"Deal," Steve smiled, and headed back to his desk.

The following day, Steve found himself actually looking forward to arriving at work. He was anxious to absorb more of Sean's insight and ultimately put his plans into motion.

As soon as Steve walked through the door, he saw Sean waving him over to his area.

"Morning, buddy," Sean greeted Steve as he approached his desk. "Do you mind if we

GETTING THE **RIGHT** THINGS DONE   39

meet right now? Just found out I have an early meeting, and I want to make sure we have a few minutes to follow up on yesterday's discussion."

"Sounds great," Steve nodded as he put his things down and pulled up a chair.

"I know we've touched on it before," Sean began, "But organization is key. I've noticed a big change in the way you keep your desk, and I'm seeing better productivity on your part because of it. Now we just need to get you to start organizing your day the way you organize your desk."

"I'm listening," Steve nodded as he took detailed notes.

Sean pulled out a sheet of paper and showed it to Steve. It had a long list of to-do items that were all checked off. Steve whistled as he went through the list. "Wow!" he said, "You sure get a lot of things done". Sean then pulled out a blank sheet of paper and asked Steve to call out items from the to-do list.

Steve called out the following
Speak to Emily about the furniture
Pick up the dry cleaning
Email the scope of work to Jerry
Speak to Jeff about the Blackberry
Prepare the Gantt chart for the Blackberry Project
Prepare the wireframes for the Blackberry Project

"Stop," said Sean as he finished writing up the tasks on the new sheet of paper. He handed it over to Steve and it looked like this:

COMPUTER	OUT
1 Email SOW to Jerry	1 dry cleaning
2 Gantt chart BB	
3 Wireframes BB	**TEAM**
	1 Ryan BB Project
	PHONE CALLS
	1 Emily furniture
	HOME

Sean explained, "If you look at my original to-do list, you will realize that it is just a huge blob of undoability."

Steve chuckled at Sean's sense of humor. Sean continued "The second list is just a way to break down my original to-do list. If you notice the left-hand column, it is much longer than the other boxes, because most of my work is done at my computer. So all I am doing is clubbing together tasks that can be performed at the same place or tasks which need the same tools like the phone or the computer. When I chunk tasks together this way, I can execute them effortlessly as I move from one task to the other."

Steve nodded in understanding. "So what you are saying is that the tasks in the left-hand column are dependent on you having access to a computer. When you are working on your computer, you can move from one task to another without interrupting your work-flow."

"Exactly," replied Sean. "It would not make much sense for me to execute tasks in a purely sequential manner, as they were listed on my original to-do list. Without a computer the left-hand column is useless - but I can still use other parts of the planner. Let's say I am waiting in my dentist's clinic for my appointment - I don't have access to my computer but I can instead do my phone calls, since I always have this list handy."

"That's why I always see you carrying around your day planner," Steve commented as he continued to write.

"Exactly. I always carry it around at the office, but frankly, I use it at home just as much. I schedule my personal life in here as well. Otherwise, I'd never remember tasks, doctor's appointments, or anything, for that matter. I also back it up with electronic reminders and schedules on my computer's calendar. That way, if I forget to check my planner, my appointments will pop up while I'm working and remind me. Speaking of which, I have a meeting reminder that's just popped up. Do you have any questions before I take off?"

Finishing up the last of his notes, Steve looked up. "I'm sure I'll have plenty once I get these plans implemented," he commented. "Thanks so much for helping me. These are some great ideas. But where can I get this day planner that you are using?"

"The beauty of this day planner is that you can make one yourself by simply drawing a line vertically down the center of a blank sheet of paper and drawing out 4 boxes on the right-hand side," said Sean.

"Ok," said Steve, "I will do that now, I'm also going to start adding things to my electronic calendar."

"Great," Sean smiled as he stood up. "I can't wait to hear how it goes."

Sitting down at his own desk, Steve began entering tasks in his planner and events into his computer. To his surprise, he felt an immediate sense of relief. Now, he no longer had to rely on his own, cluttered mind to remember every single task he set for himself or each meeting and appointment he had scheduled. It was as if someone were taking the load off of him. Steve smiled to himself as the last entry of the day he made was set for 10 minutes before quitting time.

Chapter 5

The next day Steve found himself sharing his learnings with Sean. He was happy that the previous day was much more structured as compared to his regular working days.

Sean was pleased with Steve's progress. He leaned back in his chair and his expression turned thoughtful.

"I have given you some quick wins, a few little tricks that have helped you to do some firefighting. I helped you to declutter your desk, which in turn, helped to clear your mind. Now that your mind is clear - you have gone about structuring your workday and becoming a task-master. However, this is not going to help you for very long!"

"Huh?" Steve looked up from his notepad, surprised.

Sean smiled. "Can I ask you a question?"

"Sure," said Steve.

"I gave you the book around 4 weeks ago. Why did it take you 3 weeks to read the book?"

Steve froze, wondering what Sean was up to. "I guess I got too busy!"

"Exactly," Sean continued, "Life gets in the way. You're smart enough to know that there are no 'secrets' in life. Most people intuitively know that 'exercising is good' but what they don't realize is that creating a healthy exercise routine is not really about willpower. People who rely solely on willpower fail! Sooner or later, they drop the new diet or quit the gym or go on a shopping frenzy. Similarly, you simply cannot be productive in the long term if you do not know what you want to accomplish. If you don't put first things first - life will keep throwing other things at you and you will run amok trying to get it all done."

"But isn't productivity all about getting it all done?" asked Steve

Sean replied "That's where I don't agree with all the 'productivity gurus' out there! I believe in getting the right things done, not getting everything done. I put first things first and I just drop the other things - I don't sweat the small stuff."

"But that's not what it looks like!" said Steve. "To me, it looks like you are getting it all done."

GETTING THE **RIGHT** THINGS DONE   47

Sean laughed as he replied to Steve, "Do you remember the big blob of undoability I showed you yesterday?"

"Yes, of course." Steve smiled.

"I don't prepare that list daily - I prepare it weekly," said Sean. "I do a weekly review every week, but not like the ones we do at work."

"Is it difficult to do?" asked Steve.

"Oh, it's simple," said Sean. "all you need to do is eliminate all distractions for 2 hours on the weekend. I personally prefer to go to Starbucks to plan my week ahead and look back at the week gone by."

Sean went on, saying, "I usually don't plan for a complete year - I just set goals for 12 weeks at a time. If you give yourself a year to complete a goal, you may not be able to sustain the momentum. If you give yourself 12 weeks, the enthusiasm doesn't really have a chance to die. Because you don't have time to dilly-dally around, you force yourself to get moving. Because you are monitoring your goals every week, you see immediate progress, which is enough incentive to keep going. Before you know it, you've accomplished what you set out to do. The weekly review not only ensures that you are on track, but it's also about being proactive and planning the week before it happens."

Steve was glad he'd had this conversation with Sean. Finally he had some direction. But he wondered if it was actually as simple as Sean made it out to be.

"Only one way to find out," Steve thought to himself as he sat at his desk. Sean had recommended having a broad vision with seven goals, one for each area of life, but Steve thought that having 7 goals was a bit too much; after all, he barely had any time outside of work. So he decided to begin with 3 goals for now. It wasn't difficult to decide which elements of his life were the most important and deserved his immediate attention.

His goals were as follows:

Personal

To win the 'Best Project Manager' award, which is awarded every three months

Relationships

To surprise Sue with an engagement ring on her birthday in July

Career

To get a promotion by July

Steve visualized his current reality with respect to his 3 goals. He wrote down all the reasons why he was unable to achieve those goals so far.

Winning the "Best Project Manager" award

I have been unable to do this because I have not been able to give my team effective direction and I have not even taken the time to understand the criteria that would qualify me and my team to be eligible for this award.

Getting engaged

I have not been able to do this because I have not saved up enough money, and also things have not been that great with Sue lately.

Getting promoted

I have been unable to do this because I have not been able to stand out as a leader, nor have I exceeded expectations in any way.

Looking at the goals and the reasons written out in front of him really helped Steve understand what was getting in the way of his goals. Since the next day was a Saturday, It was the perfect day to block out some time for a weekly review.

As soon as he got home, Steve packed a small bag with the following items:

Index cards
A notepad
A leather binder (to hold his index cards and notepad)
A pen
Highlighter
The book that Sean had given him

He also printed out the documents from the website which was recommended by Sean.

Printouts (documents)
Quick reference calendar
Visual tracker
7-day planner
Event planner
Process map

Steve decided that he wanted to commit to these 3 goals. While at work, he needed to focus completely on the task at hand. At home, his relationship would be his main priority. And regardless of his focus, he needed tools to keep him on track. That was where the above items came into play. Every appointment, reminder, and big event in his life was going to be written down, entered into his electronic calendar, and ultimately reviewed at the end of the week to document what went well and where improvements could be made.

Steve realized his usual routine of bouncing from task to task, leaving projects incomplete, and panicking and working late into the night when the project was due was no longer going to work. Now that he had strict deadlines for the three most important goals of his life, he knew he had to focus on each individually and get the job done. Tracking his progress was going to play a big part in his success. He made a promise to himself that he would review his progress weekly. This would offer him the opportunity to evaluate himself and decide which areas of his life required more focus in the weeks to come.

Chapter 6

Steve woke up early the next day and headed to the coffee shop for his very first weekly review. While sipping the strong brew, he opened the quick reference calendar and circled the current date, which was the 14th of April.

He noted that April 8th to April 15th was 'last week' and April 16th to April 22nd was 'next week.'

Next, he took out his index cards one at a time, to review the last week. He noted his score by shading in the corresponding number of boxes on the visual tracker for the last week as follows:

Personal – 1

Relationships – 1

Career – 3

VISUAL TRACKER

The 7 Big Rocks PRODUCTIVITY SYSTEM

1	8th APRIL TO 14th APRIL	
▮0000	PERSONAL	
▮▮▮00	RELATIONSHIPS	
▮0000	CAREER	
00000		
00000		
00000		
00000		
00000		
2	15TH APRIL TO 21ST APRIL	
00000		
00000		
00000		

Looking at his scores, Steve's spirit sank. It was evident he was not putting forth nearly enough effort in his personal life. He was falling into old habits, and he knew he needed to up his game if he was truly serious about changing his ways. "I can do this," he whispered to himself, and moved on to the next step.

He took out the 7-Day planner and started writing the date against each day of the next week:

Monday 16,
Tuesday 17,
Wednesday 18,
Thursday 19,
Friday 20,
Saturday 21,
Sunday 22.

He ensured he put dates for both the action section, as well as the appointment section of the 7-Day planner.

Looking at the event planner, Steve noted that his friend Ben's birthday was coming up on the 16th of April. He also noted his car needed to be serviced on the 20th. Steve transferred both events from the event planner into the 7-Day planner appointment section.

EVENT PLANNER

	APRIL		MAY		JUNE
1		1		1	DAVE
2		2	BETH	2	
3	NICK	3		3	TONY
4		4		4	
5		5	LINDA	5	
6		6		6	
7	SUSAN	7		7	
8		8		8	
9		9		9	
10		10		10	
11		11		11	
12		12		12	
13		13		13	
14		14		14	
15		15		15	
16	BEN	16		16	
17		17		17	
18		18		18	
19		19		19	
20	CAR SERVICING	20		20	
		21			

Since he was not able to rate any of his three goals a "5," Steve realized he needed a better game plan, and started jotting down the reasons he had been unable to make progress on his goals in his notepad. After reviewing his notes and gaining a better understanding of where he was falling short, Steve followed up with plans to help him to be more effective in attaining each goal.

Winning the "Best Project Manager" award

Action Steps:

#1. Call Sean to find out the criteria

#2. Study previous teams that have won the award in the past

#3. Call a team meeting

Getting engaged

Action Steps:

#1. Talk to Sue more often, listen closely, and nurture the relationship

#2. Earmark 50% of the money saved every week for the engagement fund

Getting promoted

Action Steps:

#1. Speak to Jeff about his expectations and ask him to review my performance with constructive criticism

#2. Speak to Sean about how I should proceed

#3. Speak to Bob about the team members' expectations

Looking at what he had just written, the wheels began to turn. He noticed that the action items he had just created for himself mostly involved getting help and feedback from others. Never before had it impacted Steve so strongly that teamwork truly was the essence of success.

Over the years, he had tried to work quietly on his own, rarely asking others for help. Evidently, this had reflected in his performance, but it took until now for him to realize it. Steve smiled to himself and shook his head. Interesting how things that he should have noticed all along were slowly coming to light.

Steve took out his highlighter and highlighted each item that could be enacted within the next week itself. He then took out the 7-day planner and noted the highlighted action items in the 'action items' section.

He figured out on which day and at what time he would be able to put each action plan into motion, and documented his plans in the appointment section of the 7-day planner. As Steve wrapped up his weekly review, he felt a new confidence about himself.

GETTING THE **RIGHT** THINGS DONE 57

Having reviewed the results of the previous work week and after setting clearer action items to assist in achieving each larger goal, Steve started the current work week with new focus and determination. As he began working on the tasks listed in the 7-day planner, he was surprised to note that he was able to finish all of his tasks by lunchtime, thereby allowing him the rest of the day to create an action plan to win the 'Best Project Manager' award.

Pleased with his progress on the first day, Steve looked forward to his next weekly review. Seeing immediate results and progress motivated him to stay on track, and he realized that at this rate, he truly would accomplish his goals in 6 weeks. Never before had he been so eager for the coming work weeks, competing with himself to see if he could make more progress than he had the week before.

The following week, Steve remembered to carry the previous week's 7-Day planner with him for his weekly review. Not only could he compare his progress more easily from week to week, but he also checked off the items that were done and rescheduled the items that were not. In addition to adding new events to his electronic calendar, he also started a new routine of setting reminders on his cell phone for all appointments and events. That way, no matter where he was, he had no excuse to forget anything.

Having developed the ability to organize his life in such a way gave him a great feeling of satisfaction, and not having to rely on memory alone put him at ease.

For the first time in months, Steve was truly happy, but nothing could have prepared him for the next day.

Chapter 7

Exhausted, Steve muttered under his breath, "Two more patches and I can be out of here by 5:45." It had been a tiring day and he hoped that it would end soon.

Fortunately, the last week had flown by, he found it easy to accomplish the same amount of work he usually did in far less time than he was used to. Not only was he more productive both at work and at home, but he found his level of stress had dropped dramatically, and he was sleeping much better these days. In fact, he found himself heading home by 5:00 almost every day in the past week.

Today was an exception, but only because one of his engineers had quit unexpectedly. The end result was that Steve had to do his own job, as well as the extra responsibilities of his missing engineer. Bob and the rest of the team were certainly pitching in, and he wouldn't have been able to do it without them, but as their manager, Steve was hesitant to burden them with much more than they could handle.

They had been so understanding during his most difficult times when he had everyone working late on a regular basis. He certainly did not wish to revisit those days, and would do almost anything to prevent more late nights for his team. "Hey Steve, what are you doing here so late?" Sean joked as he approached Steve's cubicle.

Steve smiled at the sight of his friend and mentor. "I know! It's almost 6:00! Unacceptable!" he laughed. Sean laughed along with him. "You've made some good progress, my friend. I'm absolutely astounded at how quickly you've given your desk, and yourself, an overhaul."

"Thanks, Sean. I'm shocked myself," he chuckled. "I'm so grateful to you."

Steve saved his work and locked his screen. He turned to meet Sean's eyes, and noticed a more serious look on his face than a moment ago.

"I... I have something to tell you," Sean started, anticipating Steve's reaction to his news.

Concerned, Steve felt his muscles tense. Sean was rarely this serious, and it worried him. Sean lowered his eyes and began to fiddle with the pen in his hands. "I accepted an offer for another position on the east coast today."

GETTING THE **RIGHT** THINGS DONE   61

Hearing this news, Steve felt his heart stop. He couldn't breathe. No, this couldn't be. He was making such progress with Sean as his mentor. He needed him. No...

"You know, Emily's family is back there. When we got married, I knew she'd eventually want to move back. Now with the baby coming, she definitely wants to go home. Her parents are so excited..."

Sean looked up from the pen and saw the sadness in Steve's eyes.

He placed a hand on Steve's shoulder. "Look man, you're going to be fine. Look around you. All the changes you've made in such a short time. And of course, the book is yours to keep!"

Sean smiled at Steve, hoping for some sort of reaction other than the vacant stare he was still getting. "Steve, say something."

Steve closed his eyes and shook his head. His body felt heavy, as if he were chained to the chair and unable to move. He suddenly felt very tired.

"Sean... I'm just stunned, that's all," Steve said quietly. He sadly looked around the office. "You're my best friend here, man. The one I've always counted on. Even when I was a mess, you were there. You even got me this job, remember? "

Sean looked back at the floor and nodded. "I really need to be getting back to my desk, I have some packing to do."

"I am almost done here," said Steve. "I will come over to your cube once I wrap this up."

Sean headed back to his cubicle while Steve finished up for the day.

As Steve approached Sean's cubicle for the last time, seeing the packed boxes and empty drawers as Sean checked for anything left behind, he felt his stomach drop. Sean had been an integral part of the team for such a long time, Steve wasn't quite sure how they would function without him. Stopping for a moment to take a deep breath, Steve readied himself for the occasion and continued on.

Hearing his friend's arrival, Sean looked up, smiling. "Hey man," he began. "I guess this is it." Noticing the unusual look on Steve's face, Sean's smile faded. "You ok?"

Not wanting to dampen his friend's enthusiasm, Steve tried to pull himself together and offered a shaky smile. "I just…" Steve struggled to find the words. "I'm really happy for you, Sean. Believe me, I am. You're doing what's best for your family, and that's what's important. It's just going to be very different around here without you around, that's all."

Knowing it was much deeper than that for both of them, Sean extended his hand to Steve. Steve yanked him out of his chair, and Sean put an arm around him, giving Steve a one-armed

GETTING THE **RIGHT** THINGS DONE   63

hug; the kind you usually reserve for brothers and friends you consider to be brothers.

"Well," Steve said, once they let go, "Let's get this over with." Sean nodded, and turned back to the nearly empty workstation. After grabbing a couple of boxes and waiting for Sean to pick up the last of his things, Steve put an arm around Sean as they strolled toward the parking lot together in silence.

The next few days were as difficult as Steve had expected them to be. Aside from the emptiness in the office after the departure of his dear friend and mentor, his workload had essentially doubled. Between conducting interviews for new interns and attending meetings, his own work got neglected. Since a new project manager hadn't yet been selected, Steve and Jeff had been managing Sean's team jointly, doing what they could to keep the team on track.

Fortunately, Sean's team was doing well and required little supervision. Apart from the occasional guidance required, they were pretty much on autopilot. Ryan, one of the senior engineers from Sean's old team was particularly helpful in keeping things moving forward, but Steve still felt the burden of the additional workload.

Once the weekend arrived, Steve realized that with his new, hectic schedule, he hadn't taken time out for himself the entire week. Although Saturday and Sunday would prove to be no different, he ensured that at least he would not miss his Saturday appointment with himself at the local coffee shop. Of course, even as he sipped the strong brew, he continued to monitor his work and his goals in an attempt to prioritize and hopefully maintain a semblance of balance in these difficult times.

As he noted the score against each of his goals on the visual tracker, Steve started noticing some trends. While the other two goals had been constantly improving in terms of scores, the relationship goal was consistently rated as "1" for the last two weeks. Shaking his head, he realized he had fallen into some old habits, and likely had not been appreciating Sue enough. "That's going to change," he promised himself.

Brainstorming over his latest dilemma, he decided that signing them both up for a dance class would be a good change of pace. The certain laughter accompanying the challenge of learning new moves would be a welcome addition to their relationship, and would give them a chance to reconnect. Maybe he could surprise her by leaving work early on Tuesday, and preparing her favorite dessert before she arrived home?

Finally, Steve realized that he had forgotten to carry his 7-day planner with him to the office the entire week. Without his planner, he would most certainly return to his former, scattered self. Shaking his head, he decided to start a new habit of scanning the planner after his weekly review, and emailing it to himself to prevent future mishaps. "Yes," Steve nodded to himself. "No more excuses." For the first time since Sean's departure, Steve saw a light at the end of the tunnel.

Chapter 8

Steve left the new intern alone in the conference room as his phone rang for what seemed like the 15th time that day. "Excuse me just one more time," he apologized.

Hassled, Steve stepped into the hallway and took the call. It was a call from the marketing department, asking to set up another meeting regarding the release of the new mobile app.

Agreeing to speak with Jeff and Al, Steve promised to get back to the marketing team with a date by the end of the week. Steve hung up the phone, let out a deep breath, and straightened his tie.

The new week had started out badly. The last thing he wanted to think about was another meeting. He had spent three hours this morning in an unscheduled meeting with Jeff and Al. Three hours! He was finally set free, only to be informed that Bob had called in sick, and that he would be responsible for the new intern today.

Since leaving the meeting, Steve had been working with the intern in the conference room. After almost two hours of familiarizing him with office practices and expectations, Steve was getting very impatient.

He was overloaded with his own work, and with this morning eaten up with that meeting, he felt the old, familiar stress settling in.

He rolled his head from shoulder to shoulder, stretching his neck and trying to get his mind back on the task at hand. "Ok, Steve," he said to himself, "you can do this." He headed back to the conference room to the waiting intern.

Steve had just picked up his training again, when Janice poked her head into the room. "Steve, do you have a minute?"

"Of course. Janice, this is David, the new intern with whom Bob has been working the past few days. David, Janice is an engineer on our team."

"Nice to meet you, David."

"You too, Janice."

"Steve, I was wondering if you have the discussion points from your last meeting with Al?"

"Oh yeah, it's in my bottom drawer," Steve replied.

"Let me grab it for you."

As he made his way to his desk and back, Steve couldn't help but marvel at the fact that he knew exactly where the document was, and was able to produce it in record time.

Since Sean left the office, he knew he had been backsliding a bit, but he at least he was maintaining most of his organizing skills.

Upon returning to the conference room, he saw Janice had seated herself next to David and was working with him on one of the projects Bob had given him.

"Here you go, Janice."

"Thanks, Steve. Hey, I know you're busy today... would you like me to work with David the rest of the day?"

Steve felt as if a weight had been lifted. "You have no idea how much I would appreciate that."

"No worries," she said as she led David out of the conference room. "He can sit in my cubicle with me and do his work. I'll be right there if he has any questions. Since he's an engineering intern, he may as well shadow an engineer."

"You're the best, Janice," Steve said sincerely as he watched them leave. No sooner had Steve logged into his computer than he saw a series of emails marked 'Urgent.'

"What now?" he grumbled to himself.

The first email was from Al. It had been sent to both him and Jeff. Al wanted to know the progress of another project; one that Sean had been spearheading with his team prior to his departure. Steve made a note to himself to ask Ryan for a progress report.

The next email was from Jeff. Oh no... Jeff was going to be out of the office the remainder of the day and needed Steve to meet with Martin at 4:00 p.m.

Jeff had evidently scheduled a meeting with Martin to brief him on the three hour meeting they'd had that morning. Jeff's email was apologetic; his son was sick and was at home, and his wife, an ER nurse, had been called in on an emergency. Jeff had left in a hurry to trade places with his wife, and hadn't had the time to stop and meet Steve on the way out.

His head spinning, Steve opened his notepad and began studying his notes from the meeting. Trying to remember the key discussion points, he was interrupted by Ryan, an engineer from the other team. "Steve," Ryan began, "the team has some questions about how to proceed with the next phase of our project. Do you have a minute?"

Looking at the clock and realizing he only had about 20 minutes to prepare for his meeting with Martin, he shook his head. "You know, I'm actually heading into a meeting right now," he explained. "I know you guys have been working late this week. If you plan to be here after the meeting, maybe around six-ish, I can meet with you then."

"That would be great," Ryan smiled.

As Ryan left his cube and the emails continued to pour in, Steve put his head between his hands and tried to review his notes from the meeting, but found the words ran together in a blur. He knew it was going to be a very long night.

The next two weeks went by in a flurry of work-related tasks. Even though Steve had thought that he could sign up for a dance class, there was little chance of that happening given his current schedule. He was also unable to get back home early throughout and even missed his weekly reviews because of the increased workload.

Chapter 9

As the sun began to rise through the window behind his desk, Steve glanced at the clock that now said 6:45 am. He blinked slowly, trying to soothe his dry, burning eyes.

He couldn't believe he'd been at work for over 22 hours now, and still hadn't made much headway in his work. He took a sip of his coffee which had long grown cold, and ran a hand down across his eyes, hoping to wipe away the exhaustion.

This was the third time this week he had not made it home before the sun. It's not that he didn't want to be home, but this app simply was not going to program itself.

Jeff had been breathing down his neck all week about the quickly approaching deadline for the project. This was a hell of a time to be down an engineer, but the higher-ups sure didn't seem to care about that, did they?

He didn't blame Jeff; he knew he was getting heat from Al, and he had been putting in extra hours himself. But man, these guys were expecting miracles. No matter how hard he tried, he just couldn't put his finger on the problem with the coding that his engineers had provided.

He'd had the team look at it again, and they couldn't figure it out, either. It had to be something small; a minor bug that was messing everything up.

Damn, he wished Sean were here. He'd know what to do. Actually, he knew exactly what he would tell him. He'd tell Steve to shut it down, go home and get some sleep.

As he prepared himself to run through each line of code one last time, he silently promised himself that he would take Sean's advice and go home to sleep for a few hours.. just as soon as he reached the bottom of the screen. He knew that this was a promise he wouldn't keep, but it made him feel better for the moment. As he settled back into the well-worn chair behind his desk, Steve reminded himself he had to make big changes both in the office and in his personal life.

He had been doing so well. The organized desk, the weekly reviews.. it had all started coming together. His heart sank as he thought about it. It was as if all of the progress he had made was starting to crumble. Before Sean had left, Steve had assured him he would continue what he'd started.

"Alright, snap out of it," Steve muttered to himself. He was feeling sorry for himself and he knew it. His life was nobody's fault but his own. He was making his own choices, and lately, they hadn't been good ones.

Focusing back on the screen, Steve knew there wasn't enough time to debug this messy code. He decided to rewrite the code himself and submit the app for quality testing. Hopefully it would be good enough. If not, he would be back later and could work on it then. For now, he really needed to get some sleep.

Chapter 10

The next day was no better.

"Well, team," Steve wrung his hands together as he addressed his engineers, "I know it's the last thing you want to hear, but we're going to have to make it another late one tonight."

As the team let out a collective groan, Steve raised his hands and continued his plea: "I know, I know. But headquarters has pushed up the release date on the mobile app, so we have about three weeks left to get it up and running.

"All I can say is I fully appreciate the dedication you've all shown the past several months; I do realize the toll it takes."

Exhausted, Steve retreated to his office, hearing the unhappy whispers behind him; whispers with which he had become very familiar since this project had started.

As Steve wondered for the thousandth time if being project manager was really worth it, he realized he'd better call Sue and let her know he'd be late… again.

Steve reached for the desk phone, and thought better of it. As much as he loved Sue, that temper of hers could be tricky sometimes, and he just didn't have the energy tonight.

Steve reached for his cell phone instead and started to text: "Hey, bad news. It's going to be another long night. Sorry. Hopefully the project will be over soon. See you in the morning."

As he hit the send button he heard someone clearing his throat behind him.

"Got a minute?" It was Bob.

"Oh, uh, sure." Steve put down the phone and looked up at Bob.

"What's up?"

"Look Steve," Bob began, "The team and I have been talking about the hours we've been working lately, and they elected to send me in to talk to you about it."

Wearily, Steve shook his head, knowing what was coming. "Bob, I understand everyone is overworked. Believe me, I'm right there with you…"

Bob held up a hand and interrupted, "Yes, we're all exhausted, but it's more than that. There are a lot of sacrifices being made. Paul missed his son's first high school football game last night.

"Janice had to find someone else at the last minute to pick up her kids from school both yesterday and today, and now she doesn't know who's going to watch them all night.

"We all understand the urgency of the project, but we're wondering if there's a better way to handle it." Steve nodded, open to suggestions and signalled Bob to continue.

"Maybe you could schedule late shifts on certain days. They could come in a bit later than usual and stay back late as well. That would give people time to plan and make necessary arrangements. so, I think some of this could be done from home, and brought in later for approval."

"Alright, Bob," Steve agreed wearily. "I'll definitely take a look at those options. Why don't you go around and get a schedule of which nights each person would be willing to work and we'll start with that."

Bob nodded and excused himself just in time for Steve's phone to start ringing. He reached for it, and Sue's picture appeared. "Oh boy," he thought, "Here we go." "Hi," he answered, "I guess you got my text about working late again."

Steve could hear the barely controlled anger in Sue's voice. "Steve, I don't understand. You haven't been home for dinner one night this week. How much longer is this going to go on?"

Maintaining a calm, soft voice, hoping to pass the sense of calm on to her, Steve almost whispered, "It's the same project I told you about. It's probably going to go on for 3 more weeks, or so."

Silence on the other end. Uh-oh. Sometimes that was worse than yelling. "Sue?"

When she finally spoke, her voice was strained, and Steve had the feeling she was trying to stop herself from crying, which was a bad sign.

Sue was more of a screamer than a crier, and this worried him. "It's always the same story, Steve. I don't know what to do anymore. I've been as understanding as I can, but last month you were even late to my nonna's funeral. You're putting your job above our relationship? Steve..."

Now it was Steve's turn to be silent. He didn't know what to say. She was right, and yet, he didn't know what he could say that would make any of it better.

Steve felt a lump in his throat and had a hard time getting out the words, "I don't know what to say, Sue." The silence on the line was felt like it would last forever.

Neither Steve nor Sue spoke, and after he hung up, Steve had a feeling she might not talk to him for a few days.

Chapter 11

The next day, as Steve headed to Jeff's office to talk to him about the upcoming deadline, he felt his heart begin to race and his palms grow damp.

Steve wasn't in the habit of asking for help or telling his boss he couldn't get the job done. No, Steve had always been "Mr. Reliable," the one everyone came to when they needed help.

The dependable one who everyone could count on. Lately, Steve had realized that being "that guy" just led to more work, more responsibility, and more late nights at the office. It led to stress and a damaged relationship. It led to depression.

Steve paused just outside of Jeff's office door and took a deep breath. He took a step forward, and as he was getting ready to knock, Jeff waved him in.

"Hey, Jeff. I need to talk to you about the deadline for the app project I'm working on."

Steve could hear his voice slightly crack, and he hoped Jeff didn't notice. He took another deep breath. "There's no way I can get it finished in time. I either need more people or more time," Steve proclaimed.

"I'm sorry Steve, but there's no way I can give you an extension, and there's no one left to assign to this project", Jeff responded.

Steve felt his face redden as he realized he hadn't been prepared for that response. He had given Jeff the benefit of the doubt, and had expected him to respond positively.

He froze for a moment as Jeff stood waiting for him to say something. Asking for help was new to him; being told "no" threw him completely off balance, and he had no plan B.

Not knowing what else to say, Steve turned to leave in defeat.

Jeff stopped him by asking, "Have you considered using the Eisenhower Matrix to better manage your time?"

Steve turned back to Jeff. This question intrigued Steve, as he had never heard of the Eisenhower Matrix before.

"Come on, sit down."

GETTING THE RIGHT THINGS DONE

As Steve seated himself, Jeff sat at the desk, began to draw a graph, wrote down the word 'important' along the 'Y' axis and the word 'urgent' along the 'X' axis and explained, "The first thing you'll need to do is determine which tasks are both important and urgent, which are urgent but not important, which are important but not urgent, and which are neither urgent nor important."

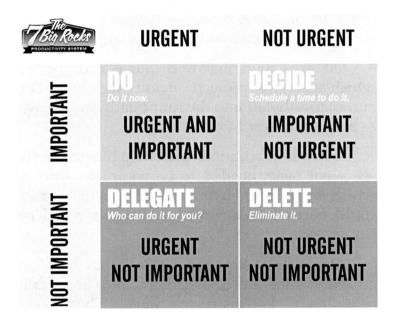

Steve listened closely as Jeff continued to explain that urgent tasks were those that required immediate action. For instance, returning an email from a client would be considered an urgent task.

Important tasks on the other hand, were tasks that needed to be completed, but could be scheduled for another time. For example, completing performance reviews for the engineers on his team was an important task, but it could also wait to be done at a later time.

Finally, Jeff continued, there were the tasks that did not fall into any of these categories, such as updating your status on your favorite social media site. Steve chuckled at that one. He knew Jeff was joking, as nobody in that office had a spare minute for something like that.

Jeff explained that once Steve had plotted which tasks fell into each category they would be automatically fall into the four quadrants known as an Eisenhower Matrix.

The four quadrants would help him to clearly see what tasks needed to be completed today, which tasks could wait for later, which tasks could be delegated, and which tasks could be eliminated.

"Begin by assigning all tasks in the 3rd quadrant that are both urgent and important to yourself," Jeff instructed Steve. "These tasks should be completed by you, today. Next, you will need to delegate all urgent, but not important tasks to your team of engineers."

"That makes sense," Steve nodded. "All important, but not urgent tasks can be set aside and completed after the project deadline.

GETTING THE **RIGHT** THINGS **DONE**   85

"Finally, eliminate all tasks that are neither urgent nor important from your to-do list. When you have completed each of these steps, you will be much better prepared to handle this project in a timely manner," Jeff proclaimed.

Steve continued to nod in agreement. "I think the trick is deciding which task is which."

"Absolutely," Jeff agreed. "If you are unsure, come see me. I can help you decide. Sometimes we think things are absolutely urgent; then we get another point of view, and realize, maybe it just isn't that serious."

"That's probably very true." Steve stood up. "Thanks Jeff, this was helpful."

"Anytime. Seriously, call me or stop by if you have any questions."

Steve nodded his thanks, and left Jeff's office feeling calmer than he had coming in. He headed back to his desk prepared to complete his Eisenhower Matrix.

He wasn't sure if the tips his boss had shared would really help, but at this point he was willing to try anything.

The important thing was that he had shared his concerns with Jeff, so if things got out of hand, at least Jeff would know that Steve had done all he could to succeed.

Steve sat down and began drawing a chart that looked just like the one Jeff had shown him with four squares, and the words 'urgent' and 'non-urgent' written at the top of the chart.

He then wrote 'important' and 'not important' vertically along the left-hand side of the chart. He began assigning each task on his to-do list to the square that corresponded to its level of importance and urgency.

All important and urgent tasks were placed in the top left-hand box, while important but non-urgent tasks went beside them in the top right-hand box.

Finally, he worked his way to the bottom of the chart placing his urgent yet not important tasks on the left, and the tasks that were neither important nor urgent on the right.

When all of the boxes were filled in, Steve was shocked to see just how much clearer his tasks had become. He was equally surprised to see how many tasks he had placed in the "neither urgent nor important" column.

Had he really been wasting so much time on frivolous things? Well, it would explain a lot... and then it hit him. The coding and debugging was urgent, but not important from his standpoint.

He really needed to move back into the project manager role and find a way to delegate this part of the work. He had an entire team of engineers; why was the project manager writing code?

Perhaps if he relieved Paul(his best debugging guy) from the day-to-day coding work and created a new role for him where he was debugging written code, that might just work!

Suddenly, Steve felt a new wave of confidence sweep over him as he prepared to once again begin work on the project. He also realized he was not alone.

He called Ryan, Bob, and Paul over to his cube, and shared his proposal. Paul was glad to be relieved of his regular tasks, and Bob and Ryan were assigned the duty of reworking the task-lists for their respective teams.

Chapter 12

After dismissing Paul, Steve sat with Bob and Ryan to estimate the time required, based on the new plan. It took a few hours, but Steve was finally happy with the new projections.

Once Bob and Ryan were gone, Steve cleaned up his workstation and headed home. In the car, he looked at the time. It was 11:38. Now Sue would be angry. Steve had been home late every night this week. He and Sue even got into a fight about it. Steve decided he would take her out on a date once this project was finished.

As Steve pulled into his driveway, he noticed the lights in his house were off. He figured Sue already went to bed. Steve walked into the kitchen and turned on the light.

He put his briefcase with work papers in it on the table. He went to get some food out of the refrigerator, but then he noticed a note taped on the front. Steve pulled it off the refrigerator and sat down to read it.

Steve,

I've decided to move out. I was going to tell you tonight, but you were late again. You promised you would stop working so late, but you still do. Every night, you're home at 10 o'clock or later. I'm tired of waiting for you to get home. I cannot date someone who loves his work more than he loves me. Please don't call or email. I need time to think.

- Sue

Gone. Sue was really gone. She had threatened to leave before, but he never thought she really would. Steve walked into the bedroom they shared and saw it was empty.

The stress at work and Sue leaving was too much for him to handle. Steve sat on his bed and broke down.

After about 15 minutes, Steve got up, picked up his car keys and drove his car aimlessly around the city, looking at the stars and hardly listening to the bad music on the radio.

He needed to be alone. At the office, everyone expected something from him. His home was empty without Sue and even though he knew where she was, he knew that he needed to give her some time to cool off.

He felt like a failure but at least the car didn't judge him.

Chapter 13

For the first time in months, Steve arrived late to work. Since most of his team members were already in the office when he arrived, he decided to call a morning meeting to address the problems they were facing.

Lately, his team had been almost as stressed out as he had been before he had decided to let go of some of his control, and delegate tasks to his engineers.

This meeting was long overdue. Steve knew one of the issues his team had was with the 15 to 16 hour workdays they had been working this week.

Unfortunately, they were starting to realize that the long days were not helping much in the progress of the project.

Despite the pressure, Steve placed a lot of faith in his team members. Above all else, he wanted to shield them from the burden placed on him. The last thing he wanted to do was cause his team to be in the same personal situation that he was in now.

As he made his way to the conference room to meet with his team, Steve gathered his thoughts, trying to figure out the best delivery. His mind kept drifting back to Sue but he had to focus on work and especially on his team now.

They needed to know how much he appreciated them, and that they could always approach him. He needed them to understand the urgency of the deadline, but didn't want them to feel they needed to work until 10 p.m. night after night.

Steve entered the conference room and looked around, noticing how stressed his people looked. "I know we are all working very hard to deliver this project," Steve began. "This team represents the future of this company. I want all of us to be here to enjoy that future.

"We have all felt it was important to go the extra mile to deliver the perfect mobile app. I see that in your work every day; in the diligence with which you work, and lately, in the long hours everyone has been putting in."

Looking at the worried faces of his engineers, Steve continued. "One of the primary reasons I wanted to speak with everyone was to review our working hours. We should not sacrifice our personal lives to complete this project. Our loved ones should be able to celebrate our success with us".

As some people nodded in agreement, others looked at him with eyes begging for answers. Sadly, Steve realized that some of them were already thinking that nothing could be done about the current situation.

Exactly the same way he used to think earlier. "We need an efficient manner of labor division," he continued. "As per Paul's suggestion, I have asked Bob and Ryan to create rosters to plan out the shifts we are working.

"This will not only ensure that everyone is given a fair schedule with no more than two late nights per week, but also that each employee is assigned the role that best fits his or her skills.

"This is the time to cater to the strength of each individual. If you are assigned a certain task, but believe you will be more effective elsewhere, please speak up. The key to success is teamwork.

"Everyone needs to feel productive; it's the only way we're going to get this done correctly, and on time."

A low buzz filled the room as people nodded and made quiet comments to each other. Steve felt he was making progress. "We will also be following the agile development methodology from now on. We're going to work in smaller teams, and each team will be cross-functional. Again, you will play to each other's strengths and adapt for each other's weaknesses."

At that, Steve took a deep breath and looked around the room. It was obvious the mood in the room had changed, and the air seemed lighter. "Does anyone have any questions or suggestions?"

To Steve's surprise, his team applauded him. He forced a smile and thanked them again for their hard work.

As the conference room grew quiet, he gave his closing remarks. "I am sure that implementing the agile methodology will ensure we can complete the same tasks within a shorter time frame. You have done a wonderful job, and I know you'll continue to do so, and I thank you for that."

As the meeting concluded and he watched his team file out of the conference room, Steve felt this was a turning point for the success of the project.

The beaming faces of his team members were a clear indicator that his ideas were welcomed, and a sense of relief permeated the office.

Steve felt a lot better now, his personal life was still a mess but at least he was on the right track as far as work was concerned.

Chapter 14

As Steve turned the key and opened the door to his house, for the first time in three days he noticed the emptiness.

It had been three days since Sue had left and moved in with her grandfather. Three days since they had spoken. She hadn't even told him she was leaving. Rather, she had packed most of her things and written a short note letting him know that he should not try to contact her.

However, what bothered Steve the most as he crossed the threshold of the empty house, was that today was the first time he was noticing the emptiness.

The past two nights, he had come home close to midnight and fallen into a deep sleep almost immediately, only to awaken at dawn and return to the office for an early start. He hadn't had the time to notice the silence, but tonight, it was too much.

Today had been different from other days. Bob had again intervened on behalf of his team, only this time, the focus had been Steve. According to Bob, the team was worried about him. They had noticed his lack of sleep in both his quality of work and in his interactions with them.

Bob had been gentle but firm when he suggested Steve cut his day short at a more 'acceptable' hour. Bob reminded him that several of the employees had been rostered to work late, and they would be fine without him.

Steve realized he was right, and left the office at 6:00 pm. Now, at 7:00 p.m., Steve flicked on the lights in the house and looked around him. Nothing but silence.

He turned back to the door, let himself out, and got into his car. He was nervous, but he knew what he had to do.

His palms sweaty, Steve noticed his hand shake as he rang the doorbell. "Who is it?" a voice grumbled from behind the door. "Vito, it's Steve."

Steve heard the lock turn and the chain unlatch as the older man opened the door. "It's about time, boy," he said as he stepped aside and let Steve in. Sue's grandfather gestured toward the couch.

GETTING THE **RIGHT** THINGS DONE   97

Steve looked at him, hesitated, but then moved slowly across the room and sat down.

"She isn't here," Vito said.

"Oh… okay, then…" Steve began to stand up. Vito raised a hand to stop him, and sat down in an old armchair.

"I know why you're here. The question is, what took you so long? It's been three days, Steve. Three days since she left. Three days since you've spoken to her," he drove the point home. "You haven't even tried to call or stop by until now."

"I know," Steve whispered. He wrung his hands together, his eyes lowered. "I… I just didn't know what to say. I didn't know how she would react or if she even wanted to hear from me."

Vito shook his head. "I know that's part of it," he began, "but I can't help wondering if you were too busy with work." Steve quickly raised his head, ready to protest, and then thought better of it when he saw the knowing look in the older man's eyes.

"It's just this project they've got me on. Jeff is adamant that we finish on time and the deadline…" Vito again raised his hand to stop him.

"I know all about the project. Sue knows all about the project. We are all so damn tired of hearing about the project, we can't hear about it one more time." He let out a long sigh. "My granddaughter deserves the very best."

Steve lowered his eyes again. "I agree, sir."

"Steve, look at me."

Steve ran a nervous hand through his hair, and slowly looked up.

What he saw in Vito's eyes shocked him. Rather than the disgust and irritation he expected, he saw wisdom and compassion.

"You're a good man, Steve," Vito began. "My granddaughter is lucky to have you. I appreciate your drive. Your ambition. You're a well-educated guy who is working hard to make his dreams come true. I never worry about Sue when she's with you. But don't you think you've forgotten something?"

Steve's head snapped up.

Seeing the surprise and confusion in his eyes, Vito continued. "You have a great vision for your life. But you've forgotten the most important things."

Entranced by the man's words and the sharing of his life experience, Steve tilted his head and listened intently.

"Love," he continued. "Family. Time for hobbies. Time for yourself. Until you add these things to your vision, it will never be complete, and the emptiness will affect every aspect of your life, including your work.

"Without balance, you have nothing. Don't you think if the rest of your life is well-balanced, you might have the ability to focus better and more completely on your work while you're there, and not have to spend such long hours at the office?"

Steve nodded his agreement, and slowly began to stand. "Thank you, Vito," he breathed. He looked down again, and then met the older man's eyes.

"Please have Sue call me when she gets in. I'll be up. We have a lot to talk about, and for once, I'm going to make sure we take the time to get it right."

Chapter 15

It had been two days since Steve had visited Vito, yet his words continued to resonate in Steve's mind: "The emptiness will affect every aspect of your life."

Since it was a Saturday and he could not bear staying at home, he had decided to come out to the coffee shop with his weekly review bag and was mulling over things with his notepad and pen over a cup of coffee.

He thumbed through the pages of the book that Sean had given him.

He mulled over two of the quotes mentioned in the book:

"It is not enough to be busy. So are the ants. The question is: What are we busy about?"

- Henry David Thoreau

"The unexamined life is not worth living."

- Socrates

He knew Vito was right, what Vito was trying to tell him was that he should have a purpose and a vision for his life. Sean had said that his vision should cover 7 focus areas and that he should have one goal for each of the seven areas of his life. He had tried to shorten the process by just having 3 goals instead of 7, but that had not worked out.

"But what should those seven areas be?" thought Steve as he went back to the conversation he had with Vito.

He noted them down the way he remembered it:

#1. Love

#2. Family

#3. Hobbies

#4. Time for recreation

He then went through his earlier weekly review sheets and noted his old focus areas:

#1. Personal

#2. Relationships

#3. Career

He figured that personal covered love and relationships covered family, but there still seemed to be something wrong. It was only when he started reading his goal for the "Personal" big rock that it finally made sense.

Personal

To win the 'Best Project Manager' award, which is awarded every three months

His life was a mess before because he had no goals apart from work. His life was a mess now because he was chasing all the wrong goals!

So he decided to replace "Personal" with "Love" and make a new list of the 7 big rocks for his life.

His new list read as follows:

#1. Love
#2. Relationships
#3. Hobbies
#4. Recreation
#5. Finance
#6. Career
#7. Organizing

To structure this newfound understanding - he decided to write out his goals for each of the 7 focus areas:

#1. Love

To win Sue back and to be more attentive to her needs.

#2. Relationships

To spend more time with the people who matter and enhance the quality of my relationship with friends and family.

#3. Hobbies

To take up golf as a hobby.

#4. Recreation

To find activities that are fun for both me and Sue which will help us rejuvenate and also keep us entertained on the weekends.

#5. Finance

To sort out my issues with my credit cards and buy an engagement ring for Sue.

#6. Career

To get a promotion by September.

#7. Organizing

To have an organized workspace and maintain a good filing system.

Steve decided to quickly get back home to get started with his 7 goals right away.

As Steve sat at his home desk, staring at the dark monitor, he realized that his 7 goals were going to be hard to chase.

GETTING THE **RIGHT** THINGS DONE 105

He leaned back in his chair and exhaled loudly. As Vito had pointed out, his life was definitely out of balance. And the more he thought about it, the more he realized his attitude toward money was at the root of it.

If he could afford to, he would buy Sue an engagement ring and ask her to marry him today. Not that he thought she would say 'yes' right now, but that had been on his mind for so many months now and he had not done anything about it.

Unfortunately, if things didn't change, he would never be able to carry out that fantasy. Work habits and poor relationship skills aside, Steve had a great deal of credit card debt.

To get approved for a loan on a ring... and yes, the ring he had in mind would require a loan... well, it wasn't going to happen with his current credit situation.

Steve had applied for a credit card when he had run into some financial difficulties a few years ago. He had been out of work for some time and at the time it had seemed like a good idea, and actually, it was. Initially, he had used it only when he'd really needed to.

It had provided a way to buy groceries and other basics when he'd been extremely short on cash.

In the beginning, he'd been doing alright with making payments; he was accruing some debt due to interest, but for the most part, each month he had been paying the bulk of what he owed.

Steve leaned his head back and closed his eyes, annoyed with himself. If he had just kept himself in check and continued that way, he would have paid off all his debt in no time.

Sue had often lectured him about his spending, but somehow he had always managed to convince her they were doing fine.

And now, years later, Steve was still in debt, and the problem was spreading far beyond just his bank account. Month after month, Steve was paying off his credit card, and once the available credit was high enough, he ended up spending it again.

He knew he was stuck in a dangerous cycle, and he was facing what seemed like a never-ending array of overdue bills.

"If I'm going to do this, I'm going to do it right," he whispered to himself as he started writing. The first step Steve jotted down was to start an emergency fund.

Steve's first thought was, "I don't have money for that.. I have to put every extra dime toward my debt or I'll never break free." Steve caught himself and put down the pen.

Taking a break from writing, he logged into his bank account. His paycheck had been deposited into his checking account yesterday.

As usual, that's where it stayed until he needed to pay bills. It would be gone soon. Meanwhile, the savings account he had opened sat steady at a measly $200.

It had been at $200 for as long as he could remember. Steve selected the 'transfer from checking to savings' option. For amount, he typed in '$1000.'

He placed the mouse over the transfer button.. and hesitated. It would leave him with barely enough to pay the bills, and certainly not enough for any extras after that. He lingered a moment longer, took a deep breath, and clicked.

Just like that, he had an emergency fund. Steve assumed his breathing would soon return to normal, but he didn't know when.

Well, since he was in a wild and crazy mood, Steve decided on something else. First thing on Monday, he was going to cash in some of the stockholder shares he had in the company.

He was going to use a bit of it to pay off some of his debt, and then... he was going to use the remainder, only what he could afford, to buy his girl a ring.

Chapter 16

Steve looked at his phone for what seemed like the 100th time in the last hour. He checked again to make sure the ringer was on. Yup, it was.

Sighing, he put the phone back down and tried to focus on watching the news, but his thoughts kept wandering back to Sue.

It had been five days since he had spoken with Sue's grandfather. He had asked Vito to have Sue call him, but his phone remained silent. Not even a text.

When he hadn't heard from her a couple of hours after speaking with Vito, he had decided to call her instead of waiting. He wasn't sure how he would be received, but he felt he should try. She hadn't picked up, so he had left a message.

When he still hadn't heard from her later that night, he'd tried again, and left another. He'd left a total of four messages in the past two days, but so far, nothing. Steve ran his conversation with Vito over and over in his mind.

Was it possible Vito hadn't told Sue he'd stopped by because he really didn't want them to be together? Or worse, did Vito tell her he'd stopped by, but changed the story, maybe telling her he had stopped by to break it off completely?

"Knock it off," Steve scolded himself. He knew Vito had delivered his message. What's more, Vito had told him he was a good man, and was happy that Steve was with his granddaughter.

Even though Steve had been lacking in a lot of areas lately and had let Sue down repeatedly, he believed the older man truly did like him, and approved of his relationship with Sue.

He and Vito had always had a good relationship, and a mutual respect of one another. No, that wasn't what had happened. Steve's mind continued to race.

Wringing his hands, he realized that if Vito had in fact told Sue to call him, and he believed he had, that meant that Sue simply didn't want to speak to him. "Geez," Steve exhaled, running a hand through his hair.

Glancing at his phone again, his heart began to race. Maybe this time she would pick up. If only he knew what Sue's reaction would be.. well, at least if he knew she wouldn't hang up on him.. that is, if she did actually pick up this time.

GETTING THE **RIGHT** THINGS DONE   111

"Alright," he whispered. "Let's try this." Steve picked up his phone and tried Sue's number. "Hi, this is Sue," a perky voice answered, "Leave me a message and I'll get back to you."

Deflated, Steve hit the disconnect button and threw the phone back on the sofa. "Now what," the thought to himself. He was out of options. Closing his eyes, he sank deeper into the sofa.

Suddenly, he felt very calm. He opened his eyes and realized what he had to do.

Digging in his pocket, he removed the princess cut diamond ring he had bought her. He turned it in his fingers, and imagined Sue wearing it. He saw her face when he knelt down and offered it, and himself, to her. He saw the tears in her eyes, and the smile on her lips.

And he knew.

Steve picked up his phone again but called another number this time. "Vito, it's Steve. I need your help."

Later that evening, Sue and Vito were enjoying a quiet dinner at their favorite Italian restaurant around the block from their house, something they tried to do at least once a week to reconnect with each other in spite of their busy lives.

"I'm glad you suggested this," Sue smiled. "I really needed an evening out."

"I know," Vito smiled as he reached for her hand. "You've been through a lot lately. We both have. Sometimes it's good to just get out, have a good glass of wine, and enjoy some good company." Sue squeezed her grandfather's hand, and took a sip of her wine. This was just what she needed right now. Peace of mind.

Sue was so busy chatting with Vito and enjoying her fettuccine that she didn't notice Steve approach their table, holding a single rose. When she looked up, anger instantly overcame her.

Sue put down her fork. "Why are you here?" she whispered angrily, trying not to cause a scene, but not quite able to keep her voice in check.

It was more of a statement than a question, and Steve suddenly had the urge to turn and walk out of the restaurant as quickly as he could. Turning red, he glanced at Vito, trying to look anywhere but at Sue. Vito looked at Steve, held his gaze, and winked at him.

"I'm going to step out for some fresh air," Vito excused himself.

"No!" Sue motioned at her grandfather as he stood up. "Nonno, please…" she begged. Vito raised a hand for her to calm down.

"I'm going to take a little walk," he repeated. "Steve," he motioned to his chair, "have a seat."

GETTING THE **RIGHT** THINGS DONE   113

And with that, Vito smiled and left the restaurant. Hesitantly, Steve sat down across from her. Sue lowered her eyes to her plate, lifted her fork, and slowly began moving what was left of her pasta around the plate.

"I've missed you," Steve breathed. "So much, you don't know."

"Steve…" she started.

"Please." Steve shook his head and reached across the table to hold her free hand. "I can never make up for all the things I've done. Not being there for you; especially at your grandmother's service. I can never make that up to you, I know. But I'm changing, Sue. I can't say I've changed, because it's a work in progress, but I'm changing. I'm working on myself every day."

Finally meeting his eyes, Sue put down her fork and sat back in her chair. "I'm listening." They talked for over an hour. He explained the progress he was making at work and the new revelations he had.

He told her how he was getting his finances under control, working more reasonable hours, and he reminded her of the good times they had shared over the years.

With that, Steve paid the bill, took Sue by the hand, and led her outside for a walk along the beach. They held hands, walked in the sand barefoot, and listened to the surf, the same way they had in the good old days.

Seeing Sue happy and smiling, Steve was the happiest he had been in weeks. He couldn't take his eyes off her. He loved the way the ocean breeze tousled her hair, the way she squealed when the cold water reached their feet and caught them by surprise.

He knew he couldn't live another moment without her. Releasing her hand, Steve stopped walking and turned to her. Sue stopped, expecting him to say something, or perhaps, kiss her.

When Steve knelt down in the sand, Sue's eyes grew larger.

"Sue," he reached for her limp hand, and held it in his own, as she stood, dumbfounded. "I have loved you for so long, and I will love you forever. You are my love, my life, my everything."

With that, he released her hand, reached into his pocket, pulled out a small box, and opened it. Sue's hand flew to her mouth, stifling a shriek of pure delight. The ring glittered in the moonlight as he offered it to her. "Will you do me the honor of becoming my wife?"

Sue, tears in her eyes and a smile on her lips, nodded mutely.

Steve again reached for her hand, and gently placed the ring on her finger as she continued to nod and started to laugh. Smiling from ear to ear, Steve stood, picked her up, and twirled her around.

This time she didn't stifle her shriek as she laughed and held him tightly, watching the world spin around her. Placing her gently back on her feet, Steve kissed her for the first time in days. It was a long, deep, precious kiss, sealing the bond between them forever.

Chapter 17

The next few days just flew by but the moment Steve walked into the office Monday morning, he could tell something big was going on.

Instead of the usual clicking of keyboards and hurried steps to and from the copy machine, a certain hush had fallen over the office.

No printers were spewing documents, and not a soul was on the phone. The only sound Steve heard was a certain frenzied whispering from cube to cube, where small groups had gathered, and seemed to be distraught over something.

Instead of walking to his desk to put down his briefcase, Steve went straight to Bob's cubicle, where Bob, Janice, and a few others were huddled together.

"Hey guys," Steve interrupted. "What's all the whispering about?" Bob and Janice looked at each other for a moment, then each turned their gaze back to Steve.

"You really don't know?" Janice asked, unable to hide her surprise.

"Know what?" Steve asked impatiently.

"Al is gone," Bob blurted out. "We've been waiting for you to come in to ask you what happened."

Steve squinted his eyes in confusion. "What do you mean 'gone'?"

"Gone," Janice repeated. "When I went to his office this morning to give him a report pertaining to the project, he wasn't in, so I decided to leave it on his desk for him. When I opened the door and turned on the light," she spread her hands in front of her, "nothing.

His desk has been cleared off; even his nameplate is gone, and everything's been taken down from the walls."

"Man," Steve exhaled, looking past Janice, and deep in thought.

"What about Jeff?" he asked, turning his attention back to Janice and Bob. "What's he saying about it?"

"Nobody's seen Jeff this morning," Bob answered.

GETTING THE **RIGHT** THINGS **DONE**   119

"But his desk is still piled high with paperwork, so no worries there," Janice half-laughed, trying to make a silly joke.

"Geez," Steve mumbled, shaking his head. As he made his way to his desk, Steve tried to process this new information, but wasn't quite sure what to make of it.

He knew Al had never been much of a leader, but to be fired... damn. And that's definitely what Steve figured had happened – there was no other explanation. To fire the Chief Technology Officer... whew, that was big.

Back in his cube, Steve tried his best to concentrate on his work. The project deadline was quickly approaching, and he knew as soon as Jeff got in, he would be all over him to get the job done.

But try as he did to concentrate, Steve's thoughts continued to wander. What if they hired a new boss who didn't like him, or thought he was ineffective as a project manager? Worse, what if he was next on the list of people to be fired?

Man, if they could fire the CTO, then nobody was off limits, right? Steve leaned back in his chair, and took a minute to pull himself together. He tried to reassure himself by remembering all the mistakes Al had made along the way. He really wasn't a good leader, and the company would be better off without him, Steve told himself.

"Ok, he wasn't horrible," Steve thought, "But what about all those late nights he forced us to work? And even with all of the extra hours, each team still missed some pretty big deadlines on his watch."

While these justifications gave him momentary comfort, Steve's thoughts quickly returned to the worst case scenario. "He wasn't really that bad," Steve mumbled to himself.

He put a hand over his mouth and closed his eyes for a moment, trying to concentrate. No matter what he told himself, he couldn't stop worrying about the future of his career.

Steve opened his eyes, lowered his hand, and straightened up. Taking a deep breath, he rolled his chair forward and turned on his computer. "Better get to work," he whispered, as he silently reminded himself of how much was riding on his current project.

He just hoped he'd be able to get at least something done today.

Chapter 18

Hey," Bob called to Steve as he walked into the office first thing in the morning, "Did you hear the news?"

Confused, Steve continued to his cubicle as Bob followed him. "What news?"

"They just announced who got the CTO job," Bob smirked, clearly enjoying himself.

Steve stopped at his desk, put down his briefcase, and prepared himself. He took a deep breath, and turned to Bob with his hands on his hips. "Ok, who got it? And how do you keep hearing all of these things before I do?"

Bob's smirk turned into a grin. "Grapevine, my man," he teased, "Gotta be in the loop around here."

"Alright, alright," Steve rolled one of his hands in the air in a 'hurry up' gesture, "Who is it?"

"Our very own Jeff!" Bob smiled. "For once, corporate made a good decision."

"Wow," Steve nodded. "Just… wow…"

Bob tilted his head and knit his eyebrows. "You don't think it's a good move?"

"Oh, no," Steve shook his head. "He's a great boss. He'll do a great job, no doubt. I'm just surprised they selected so quickly," Steve chuckled, trying to cover his true emotions. "I mean, you know how corporate works. Nothing ever happens quickly."

"You got that right," Bob laughed. "Anyway," he started to make his way to his own cube, "I figured you'd be interested."

"Definitely. Thanks for letting me know," Steve smiled as Bob left. Steve sank into his chair, and ran a hand through his hair.

He didn't know how to feel about the news. Jeff was a great boss, he thought. He had always encouraged Steve, and never missed an opportunity to let him know he was doing a great job.

Even when Steve had been struggling, and knew he was hardly at his best, Jeff still found things about his work to compliment. Steve truly appreciated all the help he had gotten from Jeff over the years.

GETTING THE **RIGHT** THINGS DONE   123

"Okay," Steve thought to himself, "Obviously this is good for Jeff." As he dug deeper into his emotions, Steve realized he really was pleasantly surprised to learn that Jeff would be the new CTO.

Of course he wanted the best for Jeff. He knew Jeff deserved the promotion; he had put in his time, worked hard, and earned it. He would thrive on the extra responsibility, and the extra money would be good for him.

So why, in the back of his mind, did he have a sense of worry that wouldn't go away? As he nervously wrung his hands together, it began to dawn on Steve. His concerns were purely selfish.

With Jeff as the CTO, it was likely someone else would be taking his place as Steve's boss. It was possible Jeff might pull double duty, but more likely than not, corporate would want Jeff to focus on learning his new job as CTO, and bring in someone else to fill his old position.

"Oh, man," Steve mumbled to himself as he ran a hand over his face. Leaning back in his chair, he tilted his head back and gazed at the ceiling.

Jeff was the only boss he'd had since he'd started here. He was by far the best boss he'd ever had. Steve knew Jeff's expectations, and more often than not, was able to meet them.

At least, that's how Jeff had always made him feel. When Jeff was around, Steve was competent.

He was appreciated. He wasn't the fumbling buffoon with the messy desk and messier life that he often felt he was. Jeff always made him feel good about his work and about himself.

"That," Steve thought to himself, "is the sign of a good boss." And not just a good boss, he realized, but a good person. A person who deserves the best, Steve acknowledged. A person who deserved this promotion, and mostly, deserved his employees to be happy for him.

Steve straightened up, turned on his computer, and sent an email to his engineers: "Let's show Jeff how proud of him we are. I'd like to plan a luncheon in his honor, to be held Friday in the break room. If anyone would like to sign up to bring a dish, I'll be passing around a sign-up sheet tomorrow. I'll also be taking donations so we can get him a small gift as a token of our appreciation for all he's done for us. Remember to congratulate him when you see him."

Steve hit 'send' and remembered something Jeff had taught him: No matter what the future held, it was going to be alright.

Chapter 19

Steve kissed Sue goodbye as he headed out the door to work. They'd had a wonderful weekend, which had turned into a joint celebration of both their engagement and the app finally going live.

Steve still couldn't believe it was over. The project that had kept him and his team in the office until late at night... the project that had almost destroyed his relationship with the love of his life.

Last Friday, the app had gone live in both the Android and iPhone marketplaces. Everyone on the team was cautiously optimistic.

Nobody knew exactly how well received it would be, but after the time and effort they'd spent, the thought of it becoming anything apart from a great success was unthinkable.

Keeping an eye on its progress, Steve had noted that throughout the weekend, the app had been downloaded numerous times. He credited this to the internal PR team who had done a great job of strategically leaking information about the app to the press.

The marketing department had done their part, posting online ads and seeding positive written reviews. Of course, Steve knew that as with all apps, word of mouth was the best promotion.

He hoped those who had downloaded it found it to their liking, and would pass the word along to their friends. After stopping at a donut shop a few streets down, Steve pulled into his parking spot, locked the car, and walked toward the building.

As soon as he opened the door, he could hear the buzz of excited voices. As he entered the office, the vibe was one of elation.

People wandered from cube to cube, smiling and congratulating each other. A sense of relief permeated the work area, and the atmosphere was more relaxed than it had been in months.

Steve smiled and greeted people as he walked to his cubicle. Bob high-fived him as he walked by. "Great job, man!" he slapped Steve on the shoulder.

"You too," Steve grinned. Relief. That was what he was feeling. Complete and total relief.

GETTING THE **RIGHT** THINGS DONE 127

Finally. Things were coming together in both his work life, and his personal life.

There was just one more thing he had to do. After calling his team into the conference room and giving each of them time to grab one of the donuts he had brought, Steve began.

"I want to thank each and every one of you for the effort you've given to this project over the past few months. From what we've seen so far, I am willing to bet that this app is going to go viral."

Looking around the room, Steve saw nods of agreement, and smiles of satisfaction. "This is a shared success story," Steve continued. "None of this could have happened without the participation of each of you. You came in early, stayed late, and gave this project 150% the entire way through.

"It wasn't easy on any of us, but you stuck with it, and with me, through it all. And now, we get to enjoy the success that belongs to all of us!" With that, the team stood up, and applauded.

Steve walked around the room, and shook each person's hand, thanking them personally for their work. "Come on," he finished up. "Everybody grab another donut and get to work. Jeff authorized a half day today, so we need to get busy if we want to move out soon!"

The staff let out a collective "whooping" sound, as they began to applaud again.

Steve smiled, headed back to his cubicle, donut in hand, and thought about where to take Sue for a date.

Chapter 20

Steve was still reeling from the excitement of the mobile app project having been completed, and the level of success it was demonstrating at such an early stage. He hadn't felt so relaxed in months. In fact, he found himself smiling for no reason at all.

"What do you think?" Bob asked, as he handed Steve the marketing report. He and Bob were in the process of wrapping up another project, so they had made their way to the conference room where they were going over the final product.

Paging through the document, Steve nodded his approval. "I think it all looks good. We should be able to have it on the market by early next week, don't you think?"

"I don't see why not," Bob agreed, as he leaned back in his chair.

"Another one down!" he cheered. "Man, we've been productive lately!" Steve smiled and was about to toss out a wise comment, when Jeff poked his head into the conference room. "Steve, can I see you in my office?"

"Of course," Steve responded, caught off guard.

Jeff turned and left the room.

"Uh-oh." Bob sat up straight and glanced at Steve with a look of concern, "That doesn't sound good."

Steve stood and gathered his paperwork. "He probably just wants an update on this project," he retorted, trying to seem unconcerned. In truth, he agreed with Bob.

Jeff looked serious, and Steve was getting more nervous by the second. "Yeah, I'm sure that's all it is." Bob turned back to the paperwork on the table and busied himself organizing the paperwork into piles.

Steve turned to the door, took a deep breath, straightened his shoulders, and walked what seemed like a very long way to Jeff's new office. As he approached the door, he took another deep breath, and gave a quick knock.

"Come in, Steve," Jeff said, almost sadly, Steve thought. "Please," he motioned toward the chairs in front of his desk, "Sit down." Jeff came around the desk and closed the door behind Steve.

A closed door meeting? Oh no, Steve thought as Jeff returned to his desk; Jeff never closes the door. Bob was right.. this can't be good. As Steve sat rigidly in the plush leather chair, he noticed the new, gold nameplate on Jeff's desk. "Jeff Gilmore, Chief Technology Officer."

It all seemed so official. The big office, the large, rich furniture... it was all a little intimidating, to be honest.

Steve had to remind himself it was Jeff sitting behind the mahogany desk. The same Jeff who had been such a good boss and friend to him. So why was Steve so nervous?

"Well," Jeff began, "I called you in here for a reason. As you know, the company has been going through some big changes." Steve nodded, not knowing where Jeff was going with this.

All he knew was that the serious look Jeff had displayed in the conference room hadn't left his face. He seemed somber in the way he kept looking away from Steve, and focusing on his hands which were linked together on the desk in front of him.

Jeff sighed. "It began with Corporate letting go of Al, as you know." Again, Steve had to take a deep breath. This was going to be bad, he just knew it. He more than knew it; he could feel it!

Steve began wringing his hands together, a flurry of thoughts taking over his mind. "They're downsizing, and I'm next on the chopping block," he thought to himself, squeezing his hands together harder.

Jeff exhaled deeply. "I suppose there's no easy way to say this." He shook his head sadly and covered his face with his hands.

"Oh God," Steve panicked, here it comes... Jeff slid his hands down his face, and looked up at Steve. "The thing is, you worked so hard on that last project, and you did really well."

Suddenly, a wide smile broke out on Jeff's face. "You've been promoted. You're taking my old job, Steve. Congratulations!"

As Jeff stood up and offered his hand, Steve was still trying to process what he'd said. "Wait..." he shook his head and slowly blinked. "What?"

Jeff cracked up and instead of a handshake, waited for Steve to stand up and gave him a hug. "I'm so proud of you, Steve. You have earned this." As it finally hit Steve, an enormous smile crept across his face. He was elated, and it showed.

"Oh my God, Jeff," he gasped, "Thank you so much! I owe my success to you. You've taught me so much. I can't wait to learn more from you."

"Absolutely," Jeff agreed. "I'll be here for you every step of the way."

GETTING THE **RIGHT** THINGS **DONE** 133

With a final handshake, Steve practically ran out of the office, in a rush to call Sue and tell her the good news. While Steve was sharing his morning with Sue, Jeff was busy sending an email out to the team, letting them know about Steve's promotion.

"He's going to be great," Jeff thought to himself as he typed. "They couldn't have made a better selection." Steve hung up the phone, unable to stop smiling. Sue had been so proud of him.

Thinking back to the years they'd been together, it dawned on Steve. Sue had never stopped believing in him. Even when they had gone through some dark times, she had still waited for him, knowing he would eventually be back on his feet.

His mind in a different place, Steve was completely taken aback when he returned to the office and his team members rushed him.

"Congratulations!" they shouted, slapping him on the back, hugging him... it moved Steve more than he could explain. These good people, who had stood by him through his most difficult times, still stood by him.

They had understood his moodiness, and had offered their help and suggestions on how to improve both his work life and his home life. Steve had to swallow hard before he could speak.

"Thank you so much... all of you," he smiled. "You are the best team, and the best bunch of people a guy could ask for. I can't wait to start this new chapter, and I'm so grateful you're all a part of it."

And with that, Steve and his crew continued to thank one another and show appreciation for the team, and the friendships they had built together.

"I can't imagine anyone luckier than I am," he thought to himself. "Tonight, Sue and I are going to celebrate like we've never celebrated before," he grinned, and mentally made a toast to them both. "Here's to the next chapter of our lives."

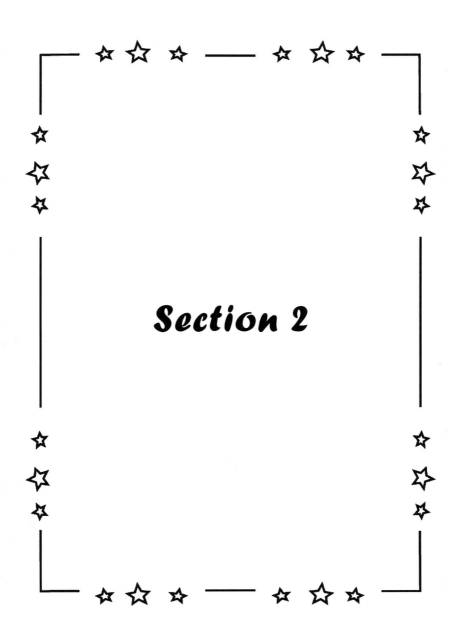

Section 2

Getting the RIGHT things done

This book is not about getting it all done. It's about getting the right things done!

Like Steve Payton, many people find themselves trapped in their crazy, busy lives. If you feel that you are unable to keep up with the fast pace of your life, then sitting in a quiet place, recording your thoughts on paper, and observing your life from an objective approach can provide a 'big picture' perspective of your current situation.

In this book I have tried to provide a framework to help you create a vision for your life — all seven aspects of it — and develop a plan for getting your life back on track. The first step of course is figuring out what the right track is.

Many people drift through life until one day something changes. It could be a personal tragedy that makes you aware that life is too short, or maybe your body feels tired and weak, giving you signals that your current pace is unsustainable. Or it could be the bank refusing your loan, or maybe your business is not doing so well anymore.

Instead of trying to figure out what went wrong, most people just try to double their efforts, but the fact is that if you don't gain control of your life using a strategic method, you might find that you never move forward. Taking control means making explicit decisions ahead of time about where you would want to spend your time and where you wouldn't.

Looking ahead a week at a time ensures that you have a solid plan to guide you, and the day planner helps you carve up your to-do list into manageable chunks giving you the flexibility to deal with a rapidly-changing world.

The idea is to check every week to see if you are in alignment with the 7 focus areas of your life. If you notice a trend where you are moving out of alignment you can correct it and get back on track.

The 7 Big Rocks productivity system

The 7 Big Rocks productivity system is a personal excellence system which provides the tools to improve your productivity, achieve work-life balance, master your time management, and achieve the results you want in your life.

GETTING THE **RIGHT** THINGS **DONE**

The best way to explain the 7 Big Rocks system is by looking at this diagram

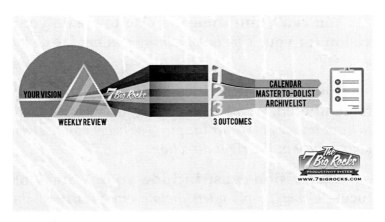

So here are the key parts of the system:

Your vision for your life: This system starts with your vision for your life, also known as your life purpose. It is represented as a ray of light entering a prism, which then breaks up into its 7 component colors – these are the 7 elements, or in other words, the 7 Big Rocks of your life. In order to achieve your vision, you need to identify goals for each of these 7 areas.

We noticed that Steve did not follow the system and tried to create shortcuts from the beginning. Instead, if you begin with a big vision for your life you will find that you can ensure that the little things go in the right direction.

> "The man without a purpose is like a ship without a rudder."
>
> —*Thomas Carlyle*

Here are some things to consider while creating your vision for your life.

You can't hire someone else to create your vision for you. *This is something you need to do by yourself.*

Your vision describes how you want to be remembered. *We all leave a legacy, whether we want to leave one or not! Your life purpose helps you to steer your legacy in the right direction.*

Your vision must include your 7 areas of focus. *Other people often dictate our priorities. By creating your own vision, you can ensure that your priorities are your own by capturing your 7 Big Rocks, or in other words, your 7 areas of focus.*

Your vision is like a GPS. *Just like a GPS, your life purpose will be your guide to take you from where you are to where you want to be in every major area of your life.*

Your vision needs to be dynamic. *You will need to tweak and adjust your vision as necessary for the rest of your life. It can be hard to create your vision for your life for the first time. But once you've done it once, you will figure that it is not so difficult to modify it the second, third, or even the twentieth time.*

Your vision has many facets. *Your vision has many facets, many different ways it could come true. Sometimes its like driving through the fog, where you are unable to see more than a couple of feet ahead of you, until one day suddenly you realize you have already reached your destination.*

The weekly review

The weekly review is represented as the prism which breaks up your vision into its component parts. It helps you review the week that has just passed by (last week) and plan for the upcoming week (next week).

Here are some tips for your weekly review.

Take stock of the current situation

Take a realistic look at what you are doing to create chaos and frenzy in your life. Examine the thinking, beliefs, and emotional attachments that have lead you to where you now are.

Envision where you want to be

Visualize the details of how the next week can contribute to your life vision. Imagine how much better your life could be and find some role models to help you change.

Go deeper to keep moving forward

Do the deep emotional work that can free you from destructive habits and emotional pain. Deepen your understanding about how you want to live and what it takes to live that way.

The 7 Big Rocks

The 7 big rocks are represented as the 7 colors which help you clarify your priorities and put the first things first. I break life down into seven essential areas that I refer to as my 7 Big Rocks.

Here they are:

Personal
Financial
Health
Relationships
Career
Contribution
Recreation

Do these seven areas cover every part of life? The answer is, of course, no, but they do cover the seven most important ones.

The first step is to identify the 'biggest rocks' in your life.

> *# Is it some pending project you'd like to complete?*
> *# Perhaps it's more quality time with your family.*
> *# Do you have a special interest of major significance to you, like certain social causes, higher education, your religion, or personal finances?*
> *# Have you always wanted to engage in a specific activity like youth mentorship or tutoring?*

As you think through your own list, here are four considerations:

GETTING THE **RIGHT** THINGS DONE 143

Your 7 big rocks are unique to you.

If you are currently single, you might not have a big rock pertaining to marriage. If you are in college, you might not have a financial big rock. What is important is that the 7 Big Rocks you choose should describe the life you want to create for yourself.

Your 7 big rocks can be named whatever you want.

Choose whatever name is meaningful to you depending on what is important to you and how narrow a focus you want. The only thing I would caution against is developing a list of more than 7 big rocks. In my experience, the individual big rocks lose their meaning when there are too many of them.

Your 7 big rocks are interrelated.

If, for example, your health is poor, it could negatively influence your marriage, your work, and possibly even your financial life. It is difficult to isolate the influence of one area from the others. Still, it is better to list them, so that you can give the appropriate amount of attention to each.

Your 7 big rocks will change over time.

I have updated my 7 big rocks regularly over the years. The important thing is to develop a list that reflects your current reality.

I would like to give you two ways other people have categorized their own 7 big rocks:

Example 1 - By Role:

Father
Husband
Brother
Son
Manager
Friend
Mentor

Example 2 - Alternative Categories:

Mind
Body
Productivity
Organization
Finance
Relationships
Fun

Now it's your turn. Grab a pen and paper and jot down your own 7 big rocks. You can use these lists as a guideline or create your own.

The Outputs

There are 3 outputs of the weekly review.

Output 1 – The Calendar - calendar items are tasks/events that are date or time sensitive.

Output 2 – The Master to-do list. (Also known as the 7-day planner)

Output 3 – Archive List.

Daily Checklist

Using the calendar and the master to-do list you need to make a new work list each day. Identify 3 outcomes for the day. One simple way to figure this out is to ask yourself what are the 3 most important things to accomplish today? Having a simple set of 3 outcomes will guide all your activities. While executing them, ensure that you first execute the activities that will take you towards your 7 goals before you execute anything else.

The Why Behind the Approach

3 reasons that make this approach effective:

1. It's simple, manageable, and easy to understand

2. The core idea is about designing your life rather than just becoming a task-master.

3. These methods can be applied to your life right away with the overall systemm helping you create productive habits for yourself.

Vision

In his book The 7 Habits of Highly Successful People, Stephen Covey describes the funeral exercise. In the funeral exercise, he asks you to imagine attending a funeral and recognising many of the people in the church, and then when you peek into the casket, you come face to face with yourself. Yes, it is your funeral, 5 years from today!

Picture three people getting up to say a few words about you, the type of person you were, what you stood for, how you lived. The first speaker is a good friend or family member. The second is someone from your community. The third is a work colleague.

He then asks you to close your eyes and imagine all three speakers giving sincere and glowing testimonies of you and the life you lived. Everyone listening is moved to tears as they remember how much you meant to them, noticing that the world is a little less bright now that you've gone.

He then asks you to open your eyes and figure out what it is that you want to be remembered for by your friends, colleagues, family, and everyone else.

Three Powerful Questions

It all boils down to answering three powerful questions:

Question 1: How do I want to be remembered? How would those closest to you summarize what your life meant to them?

Question 2: What matters most?

Question 3: How can I get from here to where I want to be?

I am also going to ask you to start dreaming specifically about who you want to be in five years. Why five years? Five years is small enough that you can get your mind around it. It doesn't feel too far away. It's also large enough that a person with the right effort can genuinely make a change in their life for the better.

Now, what are you going to dream about? I want you to think positively about the new you, the new attitude, the new title, the new salary, the new responsibilities. What are you going to be?

GETTING THE **RIGHT** THINGS **DONE**   149

You will need to be specific. As you start to articulate these future states that you wish to achieve, don't allow your thoughts to dissipate. You've got to capture them, and write them down, either on a pad of paper or on a computer. Make sure you securely capture them so you can go back and reflect on them and what they mean to you.

There are four reasons to envision what you want.

First, imagining a different future helps you believe that it is possible. The very act of imagining something different in your life starts to create new neural pathways in your brain. The new image prepares you for change. At first it seems impossible, then over time, step by step, visioning brings the impossible first into the realm of possibility and then into the realm of likelihood. Visioning is like tilling the soil; it prepares your heart and mind for something new.

Second, as you keep envisioning what you want, you identify your vision as something you want for yourself rather than something dictated by other people. Knowing your purpose and clarifying your vision strengthens this voice. People often identify this voice as a voice of external authority that is telling them what to do. They don't want to obey that 'bossy' voice, so they don't do what it is asking. But through visioning, you can re-identify that voice with your own inner strength and recognize that it is encouraging you to get what you really want in life. Making this shift is essential to increasing your sense of inner authority and well-being.

A third reason for envisioning what you want is that it helps you see where you are. You may be living more of your vision than you think, but you won't know that until you explore what your vision really is. Visioning shifts your mindset.

Finally, once you imagine what you want, you'll start to see ways to go after it. Your vision helps you tap into your goals. Your subconscious mind will register things differently. It will start to identify patterns in the environment around you and focus on things that will take you closer to your vision. It will identify things that were always there, but which you never noticed them because you were not clear about what you wanted.

You Could also Start with What You Don't Want

If you can't imagine what you do want, maybe you could try starting with what you don't want. "I don't want my desk to be so cluttered." Then, you can go on from there. Ask a few questions: What would it be like if you didn't have the piles? What would you get if you had clear spaces? What would it look like? What would it smell like? What would it feel like?

Write down your vision of the details in your life with as much vividness and precision f possible. You will use this description every day to remind yourself of where you are going.

An Example of a Vision Statement

I sleep easily knowing that my to-do lists are complete and I am productive. I awaken refreshed. I exercise daily and keep myself fit. I have a list of things I need to do tomorrow. I have a trim and healthy body and I am feeling light and alive at my perfect body weight of 135.

I arrive at work on time. My workspace is energizing and organized. I have the right work environment that I need here. My work surfaces are clear. I can lay my hands on whatever I need, whenever I need it. I spend time focusing on my priorities. I say yes to what I can do, and no to what I cannot do. My skills are in demand in the marketplace. I feel great about being on top of things.

I have a good system for tracking my money. I know where my bills and financial documents are. I know what I owe, and my money is under control. I sit down twice a month to make investments. I care for the money I have, and I keep track of both the money that I bring in and the money that I spend.

I walk into my home at the end of the day and I immediately feel refreshed and relaxed. Our home is a place of peace and love. It is a sanctuary, a haven. I love the beauty that surrounds me. This space completely supports me and my family to live well.

Choose your vision again. Choose it every day.

The Weekly Review

One of the most important things you need to do is to plan ahead using weekly reviews. Do not neglect this step, because it is essential for becoming more productive. Plan ahead and schedule checkpoints to make sure you stay on course toward success. I have created a complete weekly review system, which is available free of cost on my website. You can download the complete system here:

http://7bigrocks.com/7

The Outputs

As mentioned earlier, there are 3 outputs of the weekly review. The first is calendar items which are things that are date or time sensitive. The second is your master to-do list and the third is the archive list

Output 1 : The Calendar

If you need to do a task that is date-sensitive or time-sensitive, that becomes a calendar item for you because you need to enter it into your calendar so that you don't miss that time or date. A good example is a birthday - it is better to wish someone on their actual birthday itself rather than wishing them a day later. So if you forget to put a reminder on your calendar you are likely to forget their birthday because it is date-sensitive.

Output 2: The master to-do list. (Also known as the 7-day planner)

Do you sometimes feel that 24 hours in a day is not enough for you to get everything done? You are not alone – most people feel that they can't finish their tasks for the day and so they feel discouraged. The fact is that while there is never enough time to do everything there is always enough time for the most important things (which are your 7 Big Rocks). It has also been noted that most people overestimate what they can do in one day but they tend to underestimate what they can do in a week. This master to-do list helps you keep track of all the things you need to achieve during the week. Please note that the master to-do list is not for date-sensitive or time-sensitive tasks, those would qualify as calendar items – so you need to move those over to your calendar as we discussed earlier.

Output 3: Archive List.

When you are doing your weekly review and you notice that you keep delaying certain tasks or procrastinating on them – you need to move these tasks onto your Archive list. Another good reason for moving tasks to your Archive list is that you simply would not be able to tackle those tasks in the next 7 days – that is a perfectly valid reason. So you are simply storing these tasks on the archive list instead of burdening your mind with them.

Here you are making a conscious decision that you would get to these tasks on a later date and not cluttering your mind with additional tasks that you genuinely don't have the time to take care of.

This list can also double up as a reference list to free up your mind by creating a place to look for your reference information – the idea being to separate your action lists from your reference list.

Tips for Creating Your Plan

1. Keep a record of everything.

2. Know what you want to do.

3. Be specific and realistic in your planning.

4. Set measurable milestones.

5. Break large tasks into smaller, more manageable chunks.

6. Make a list of tasks that you need to complete in order to hit your milestones.

7. Put timelines on everything.

Tips for Managing Your Time

1. Use the day planner provided at http://7bigrocks.com/7

2. Do less - focus on your 7 Big Rocks - the things that matter before you do other tasks.

3. Learn how to time block.

4. Schedule time for leisure and breaks.

5. Disconnect. This includes turning off your phone, if possible, at least for periods where you really want to focus on work.

6. Know what a sample scheduled day looks like - create an ideal day or an ideal week as a reference point.

7. Schedule for problems.

The Daily Plan

The key to more productivity is not only time management but also having the right work strategy. Scientific studies have shown that the more information we try to store in our brain at once, the less of it we will remember. It is not only things related to work that we have to remember, but also personal obligations. To make your brain function better, you have to rewrite your to-do list, sort your tasks, and get rid of the ones which are not important.

The best way to do so is to create a master TASK list, by following the steps Think, Ask, Sort and Keep.

Think

First of all, you have to dump all the things that are stored in your brain and put them in a physical form. Think about everything you need to do and write it down. This helps you get the thoughts out of your head and down on paper.

Then think of all the steps you will have to take to achieve that goal. This way, your mind will become free to think again.

Act

When you look at the results of your brain dump, you might notice that most of the things you listed are projects rather than actual to-dos. Projects may require a number of steps, while to-dos are much clearer, so try to define concrete action steps for all the items on your list.

Sort

Your list of necessary steps will most likely be chaotic at first, so the next step in the process is to organize it and prioritize certain actions.

Keep

This stands for "keep only one list," to make sure that everything you need to do is gathered in one place, which will make it easier for you to keep an overview and make decisions regarding what has to be done next. Keeping more than one list will only create confusion and most likely result in wasted time.

The way in which your daily plan takes shape will depend on your style. Perhaps you like to write everything down in a day planner to help you keep track of everything you have to do. Or maybe you prefer an online to-do list that allows you to access it from any computer. It doesn't really matter how or where you keep your plan as long as you are able to access it easily and quickly when you start working.

In the story, Sean showed Steve how to break down his original to-do list. The basic idea was to group all activities that were to be performed in the same location together. The left-hand column was the longest column on the sheet, so it was used for computer-based tasks. Some people prefer to use the left-hand column as a master to-do list and the other four boxes on the right hand side for clubbing together outdoor chores, phone calls, emails, and home.

It does not make sense to execute tasks in a purely sequential manner, as they are listed on your master to-do list. Doing your to-do list in this manner also helps you de-clutter your mind, not just your to-do list.

Once you have the format for your daily plan, set a timer before you start acting on your tasks for the day. This will keep you from getting distracted. Remember, the goal is to get you to be productive in chunks, so make your goals realistic. Focus on small tasks that will eventually add up to bigger projects. For example, if your eventual goal is to get your books balanced, your initial task can be downloading and categorizing the bank transactions for the first month. You will be amazed at how many of those smaller tasks you can get done in just 10 minutes every day! They really add up and before long, you will see how much better you can manage your bookkeeping tasks.

Key Concepts

Managing your attention

Interruptions are common in our working life. We are constantly interrupted throughout the day by colleagues, emails, or other distractions. All of these things demand our attention and force us to take our attention away from the tasks we really should be doing, thus lowering our productivity. To be more productive, we have to decide when to pay attention to them and when to choose to focus on the tasks at hand.

Most workers can only focus for 3 to 15 minutes before they are interrupted. After such a distraction, it can take them more than 20 minutes before they are able to fully focus on what they were doing again. However, distractions are often seen as necessary, because we have set expectations that we will reply to emails or messages within a few minutes or even a few seconds.

There are two types of attention: voluntary and involuntary. The first one is triggered by influences from outside. Earlier, our sense of survival alerted us to always watch out for threats. Now we are mostly concerned with meeting the demands of our superiors or co-workers, but we are unable to distinguish between the signals that go off in our brain in response to a wild animal and the sound that tells us we have received a new message.

Stop reacting and start responding. Don't let technology control you. Instead, you should take control of it by setting certain times for checking emails or messages and not letting yourself get distracted by such interruptions. Knowing that a lot of new emails will have accumulated every morning when we get to work can put a lot of pressure on us and make us dread opening our inbox. Since they can be sent from anywhere and at any time, we cannot even escape from them in the evening or on the weekend.

You don't have to start every day by checking your emails. Many people even consider it wrong to do so. Instead, make it a habit to work on your most important task first thing every day, because the morning hours are usually the most productive time.

Another practice that should be eliminated is checking your inbox every few minutes for new messages. This is an ineffective use of your time, so try to keep those checks to once an hour and focus on the tasks at hand in between. An even better method would be to assign certain times to checking emails, such as mid-morning, after lunch and mid-afternoon.

If something is really urgent, people can still call you directly on your phone, so you probably won't miss anything important. People you frequently correspond with might also change their habits as a result and be relieved of some of the pressure of always having to reply instantly.

Managing your energy

It is so easy to get caught up in the race for success, the juggling act of family, work, and play, and just staying one step ahead of everything. The busyness depletes your energy and makes you lose focus.

You expend far too much energy making unrealistic plans, hunting for lost objects, scrambling to meet deadlines, and apologizing for being late. You end up running on empty because you exhaust your reserves as you deal with the impact of your own chaos.

Physical activity is one way to get rid of negative energy and it also creates energy reserves for the rest of the day.

Invest your time wisely: take a close look at your schedule and make sure that none of the activities listed there take time away from you. All of them should contribute to achieving your final goal.

Ask for help: don't think that you have to do all the work by yourself. People are often happy to help, so don't hesitate to delegate some tasks to others.

Managing your focus

Get clear: find out what is holding you back and eliminate it. Often, you are unable to see clearly because something is obstructing your view. Get rid of it to achieve more personal freedom and become creative.

Embrace your productivity style: there is no single approach that will work for everyone, because each person has their own style and needs to match their techniques and tools with it in order to work productively.

Know where you want to go: don't decide your goals based on what others want you to do. Think about what you want for yourself and prepare concrete plans for achieving it.

Meetings can take up a lot of time, so you should only attend them if you think they are really necessary for you to get closer to your goals. Each meeting should also have a clear agenda to make sure it can be started and finished within the allotted time and produce the desired results.

To increase our brain's ability to resist distractions, we have to strengthen our focus. The first step to do so is "cultivating awareness".

Over a period of around four hours, write down what distracts you. This exercise enables you to see how often your mind wanders and what has the greatest influence on you. You can then start to look for trends, such as times when you are more easily distracted.

The second step in this process is "optimizing the environmental factors". This means to adapt your environment in such a way that makes it easier for you to focus, by eliminating as many distractions as possible. Generally, desks should be kept as clutter-free as possible and we should get rid of things we don't need right away. If you have the luxury of a cabin, close the door. If you have the option of choosing a cubicle, choose one that faces a wall or simply invest in noise-cancelling earphones. If these steps seem too drastic, consider the alternative – you'll be constantly disturbed by other people.

Getting Ready

Now here is a complete system. This system is everything you would ever need in order to be productive. "Really?" I hear you ask.

I'm sure that this system works, for the following reasons:

1. *I have tried it myself.*
2. *It is a flexible system and does not require fancy templates and apps.*
3. *It integrates tasks with your goals and focus areas.*
4. *It allows you to easily organize and plan your weekly and daily responsibilities.*
5. *It is compact, simple, and efficient.*
6. *It is a modular system and does not depend on a particular sequence of activities.*

Even though I stand by my reasons, I am fully aware that this system could fail. This system could fail if any of the following hold true:

1. *You love to multi-task.*
2. *You have a short attention span.*
3. *You are too comfortable.*
4. *You are not a planner.*
5. *You love to keep tweaking and looking for other systems and trying to mix them up.*
6. *You are just not ready!*

While I would love to believe that I could help you, I guess the only condition where I can help you is if you are not yet ready, but want to be!

As Steve Payton realized, in order to be productive you need to be organized and have an organized workspace. Many people are buried in a backlog of email, clothes, special mementos, or old furniture. Their backlog hangs over them as they live their lives.

They are not mentally ready because they can't find things, don't feel comfortable at home or work, and don't use their space well. Too much of their home or office has become dead storage. The drawers, the closets, the attic, and the garage that are filled with unusable clothes and old sporting equipment are all daunting. It will take several days to get through it, if not months!

'Getting ready' does not have to mean creating immaculate order. It will be different for each of us. Some people will feel a sense of readiness when they know where their keys and glasses are. Others won't feel they are ready until the desk is totally clear, all previous work is filed, and all phone calls are returned.

There is a feeling of fundamental ease at "ready," because you can find things and you're not overbooked. Being productive and organized is not about having alphabetized or color-coded folders. It's not about neatly arranged furniture or neat piles of papers.

Being organized means:

You can find what you want when you need it.

You can keep track of important information and lay your hands on it when you want to.

You can complete your tasks in a timely way.

You can keep agreements and make agreements that you can keep.

You can take action when you want and seize new opportunities as they arise.

You can focus on what is important to you.

You can do all of this with a great degree of presence of mind.

You are able to pay attention to what you decide is important.

Once your desk is clear, your belongings and laundry are put away, and your schedule is manageable, you feel ready to do what you want to do. Getting ready is a change of mind and focus. As we put things away and finish off the day or the week, we can see that we are more available for what is to come.

How Much Breathing Room Do You Have?

Maybe you've said something like this to yourself or your spouse:

"As soon as I settle in to this new job, I will have some breathing room."

"As soon as I get this promotion, I will have more time to do other things."

"As soon as the kids leave home for college, I will have some time for myself."

But before you know it, weeks turn into months and months turn into years. People go from one '"temporary situation' to the next. Before long, it's permanent. What we desperately need is a margin — some time to breathe, to reflect, to act.

The weekly review is the best time to plan for a margin and it gives you the space to think and reflect on the previous week and plan for the next week.

Set Good Boundaries

Some of us believe that saying no, setting limits, and expressing our own limitations is risky or selfish. So people often set their limits, say no, or express their dislike with a situation not through an intentional statement, but through their disorganization. Running late, being overbooked, forgetting commitments, not returning phone calls or e-mails, being incredibly stressed, cancelling at the last minute, or having a desk that is piled high with papers – all of these are ways of being unavailable, without directly saying no.

You might feel that you are putting relationships at risk by being direct about what you can, cannot, or don't want to do. Yet you are putting relationships at risk anyway with your high-stress 'Now you see me, now you don't' disappearing act. Maintaining personal boundaries involves making clear requests as well as clear responses to requests.

When someone makes a request, don't say yes immediately. Try saying, "Can I get back to you on that?" This is hard when you feel that urge to say, "Yes, I'll do it." Then make sure that you do get back to that person within a reasonable amount of time.

Don't say no by disappearing. Make it a practice to imagine how exactly you will do what you promised. Consider if the deadline is reasonable. Check your calendar to see if you have time to keep your agreement.

Learn what a manageable deadline is. Next, get to know why you have trouble with saying no. Are you afraid that you won't be valued if you set limits? Are you concerned that you won't be seen as a team player? Are you nervous that others might see you as selfish or weak?

Often our reasons for taking on too much are not tested. We just load up our schedules and then pay a very heavy price for it. Sometimes, you think you can't say no to someone, but you might start to recognize that your outward busyness may just be an indirect way of saying no.

Conclusion

There's so much advice out there, and some of it seems to be contradictory! With this book I have stripped away the non-essentials and tried to give you a framework that you can apply to any situation. I'll leave the 'deciding' part up to you!

You've now learned the entire system — what it is, why it works, and how it works. Now, it's time to put it to use in your own life and business.

To help get you up and running quickly, here's a simple three-step action plan:

Step 1: List down 7 goals one for each area of your life

Step 2: Follow the 7 Big Rocks productivity system even if you are unsure whether it would work for you.

Step 3: Review what worked every week.

There may be setbacks, but there are also solutions to the problems that arise. With some dedication, motivation, and a disciplined approach, you will be able to bounce back from any setback.

I wish you all the best in your life journey!

Your Free Gift

As a way of saying "thanks for your purchase," I'm offering a free download of my ebook 'Wake Up Successful - How to Increase Your Energy & Achieve Any Goal with a Morning Routine.'

Getting unstuck is a real problem for a lot of people. The trick is to identify what you need to get done and create a step-by-step strategy to launch your day so that you execute your tasks in the most efficient way possible.

In 'Wake Up Successful,' you'll discover several ways to launch your day with a tried and tested morning routine. This will enable you to make lasting changes to your work, success, health, and sleeping habits.

You can download this free ebook by going to the following webpage:

http://7bigrocks.com/mr/